## At Issue

| Alcohol Abuse

# Other books in the At Issue series:

# At Issue

## Alcohol Abuse

*Ronnie D. Lankford, Book Editor*

**GREENHAVEN PRESS**

*An imprint of Thomson Gale, a part of The Thomson Corporation*

Detroit • New York • San Francisco • New Haven, Conn. • Waterville, Maine • London

Christine Nasso, *Publisher*
Elizabeth Des Chenes, *Managing Editor*

© 2007 The Gale Group.

*For more information, contact:* Greenhaven Press
27500 Drake Rd.
Farmington Hills, MI 48331-3535
Or you can visit our Internet site at http://www.gale.com

**LIBRARY OF CONGRESS CATALOGING-IN-PUBLICATION DATA**

Alcohol abuse / Ronnie D. Lankford, book editor.
    p. cm. -- (At issue)
    Includes bibliographical references and index.
    ISBN-13: 978-0-7377-3671-7 (hardcover)
    ISBN-13: 978-0-7377-3672-4 (pbk.)
    1. Alcoholism--United States. 2. Youth--Alcohol use--United States. 3. Alcoholism.
    4. Drinking of alcoholic beverages. I. Lankford, Ronald D., 1962-
    HV5292.A374 2008
    362.2920973--dc22

                                                            2007024134

ISBN-10: 0-7377-3671-2 (hardcover)
ISBN-10: 0-7377-3672-0 (pbk.)

Printed in the United States of America
10 9 8 7 6 5 4 3 2 1

# Contents

# Introduction

## Why Do Adolescents Abuse Alcohol?

A lcohol is the most widely abused drug in the United States, and is both legal and readily available. "Most people consider alcohol a normal part of the culture in Western societies," writes Cynthia Kuhn, Scott Swatzwelder, and Wilkie Wilson in *Just Say Know: Talking with Kids About Drugs and Alcohol.* "We use alcohol to celebrate, worship, relax, and commiserate." Alcohol is also directly and indirectly responsible for individual and societal problems ranging from poor performance in school to automobile fatalities. According to the American Medical Association (AMA), 11 million Americans under 21 drink alcohol; half that number drink "five or more drinks in a row," behavior that is now commonly defined as binge drinking. The AMA also states that nearly half of teen automobile fatalities involve alcohol and that alcohol is involved in two-thirds of sexual assaults and date rapes.

Despite these dangers, teenagers and young adults under the legal drinking age continue to abuse alcohol. "Warnings against underage drinking from parents or in health class may well be drowned out by the barrage of daily messages about alcohol in daily life," writes the National Research Council/ Institute of Medicine in *Reducing Underage Drinking: A Collective Responsibility.* Teens abuse alcohol for many reasons including curiosity, mood alteration, and relaxation. "Kids are naturally curious," writes Kuhn, Swatzwelder, and Wilson, "and as teenagers they are in a lot of emotional pain." Reasons frequently overlap and may be influenced by friends, family, and genetics.

## Peer Pressure and Advertising

Peer pressure has been cited as an important component in youth alcohol abuse. "Peer affiliation and desire for peer acceptance are hallmarks of adolescents," writes H. Thomas Milhorn, Jr. in *Drug and Alcohol Abuse: The Authoritative Guide for Parents, Teachers, and Counselors*. While peer pressure is often thought of as friends convincing one another to participate in risky behavior, individuals often generate peer pressure from within. "At almost every party a high school student attends, there is alcohol," writes Brady Ruebusch in *Mountain View Voice*. "Many students drink at these parties because they don't want to feel left out. . . ."

Advertising has also been cited as influential in promoting underage alcohol abuse. "The high levels of exposure to alcohol advertising for youth in general, and for girls in particular, are cause for concern," Jim O'Hara, the executive director of the Center on Alcohol Marketing and Youth, told *JustDrinks.com*. Alcoholic advertisements are prevalent in all media outlets (television, radio, the Internet, newspapers, and magazines). Alcohol advertising has also become prevalent in sports. Anheuser-Busch sponsors NASCAR's Busch Series; in European rugby, Heineken sponsors the Heineken Cup. Other critics have pointed to specific alcohol products like alcopops—sweetened, pre-mixed drinks like Smirnoff Ice and Bacardi Breezer—as products that are specifically designed to appeal to a youth market.

## Personality Characteristics and Risk Taking

Researchers believe that certain personality types are more likely to abuse alcohol than others. One example is adolescents with ADD (Attention Deficit Disorder) or ADHD (Attention Deficit Hyperactivity Disorder). "The researchers found that individuals with severe problems of inattention as children were more likely than their peers to report alcohol-related problems, a greater frequency of getting drunk, and heavier and earlier use of tobacco and other drugs," concludes an *NIH News Release*. Youths suffering from anxiety and depression are also more likely to abuse alcohol, though researchers remain uncertain on one important factor: does anxiety and depression lead to alcohol abuse, or does alcohol abuse lead to anxiety and depression?

Other youths who abuse alcohol seem to have a greater propensity to risky behavior. "Students who have higher needs for sensation seeking are more likely to report higher levels of drinking, as well as other delinquent behavior," writes the National Research Council/Institute of Medicine. Furthermore, youths who seek risky behavior may associate with other sensation seekers, increasing the likelihood of aberrant behavior. Other behavior problems have also been connected to alcohol abuse. "Children classified as 'undercontrolled' (i.e., impulsive, restless, and distractible) at age 3 were twice as likely as those who were 'inhibited' or 'well-adjusted' to be diagnosed with alcohol dependence at age 21," notes *Alcohol Alert*.

## Family Influences and Genetics

Youth who have an alcoholic parent are influenced in a variety of ways. "The example set by parents with their own drinking has been shown to affect their children's drinking throughout their lifetime," notes *Alcohol Alert*. Children develop attitudes about drinking from watching parents and adults; if these authority figures express a positive attitude toward drinking, children may develop a similar attitude. Likewise, a child may be less likely to accept a parental figure's warnings against the dangers of alcohol abuse if that parent also abuses alcohol.

But the potential for alcohol abuse also has a genetic link. "Research has shown conclusively that familial transmission of alcoholism risk is at least in part genetic and not just the result of family environment," notes *Alcohol Alert*. With these multiple environmental and genetic influences, the chance that a child of an alcoholic will also have an alcohol abuse problem increases dramatically. "Children of alcoholics (COAs) are between 4 and 10 times more likely to become alcoholics themselves than are children who have no close relatives with alcoholism," notes the National Institute on Alcohol Abuse and Alcoholism.

## Society and Alcohol Abuse

Education pertaining to alcohol abuse has often focused on its dangers. In literature concerning binge drinking, many writers emphasize the number of deaths that result from alcohol poisoning each year among high school and college students. In literature concerning traffic fatalities, many writers concentrate on the number of deaths caused by underage drunk drivers. The reality of these statistics may be self-evident, but many adolescents will choose to abuse alcohol regardless of grim realities.

Observing the reasons why adolescents abuse alcohol offers another educational opportunity for both adults and adolescents. It offers a chance for adults to remember the pressures that a teen faces in his or her daily life; a chance to understand why a teen might be tempted to participate in a potentially dangerous pastime. It also offers an opportunity for adolescents to attempt to comprehend and question their own behavior. By understanding that the primary purpose of an alcohol advertisement is to sell a product, adolescents can separate fact from fiction. By understanding how family history or personality characteristics may affect one's reaction to alcohol, adolescents can assess the risk involved. This knowledge empowers adolescents to make the choices that only they, ultimately, will have to make.

# 1

# Moderate Alcohol Consumption May Provide Health Benefits

*Hillary Wright*

*Hillary Wright is a founder of New Vision Nutrition and a nutrition educator for the Dana Farber Cancer Institute in Boston.*

*Many researchers believe that alcohol, when consumed in moderation, has health benefits. These benefits may raise "good" cholesterol, decrease the likelihood of diabetes, help avoid obesity, and reduce the cell damage that leads to cancer. Health benefits, however, can also be achieved by eating foods and drinking beverages that—like red wine—are rich in antioxidants (fruits, vegetables, and green or black tea, for example). The benefits of alcohol are quickly voided with excessive use: The key to alcohol as a health aid is moderation.*

The purported health benefits of red wine have reached near-legendary status. The theory that it benefits heart health was bolstered in the early 1990s by research that found that the French had low rates of cardiac death despite their well-known penchant for fatty foods. Dubbed "The French Paradox," the findings prompted much research and considerable debate.

Researchers initially attributed French heart health in part to potent antioxidants in the red wine they've enjoyed for centuries. But more than 10 years and numerous studies later, most researchers believe it's likely the alcohol that's responsible for most of the cardioprotective effects of wine. That means beer, wine and spirits should have equal potential for benefiting your heart—*when consumed in moderation.*

All experts agree that drinking too much of any kind of alcohol is not healthy. Period. Clearly, people who cannot limit their intake should not drink. Others who should avoid alcohol include anyone driving a vehicle, those who are pregnant or breastfeeding and people taking certain medications or with specific health conditions.

---

*All experts agree that drinking too much of any kind of alcohol is not healthy.*

---

Given those caveats, *EN* [*Environmental Nutrition*] looks at the pros and cons of alcohol use to help you decide what's right for you.

## Alcohol's Pros and Cons

*The Heart of the Matter*

*Point:* Most evidence in support of moderate alcohol use comes from cardiovascular research. According to alcohol researcher Eric Rimm, Sc.D., of Harvard's School of Public Health, "about 50 randomized studies show that when consumed in moderation, alcohol increases high-density lipoprotein (HDL or 'good') cholesterol and decreases blood clotting and insulin resistance—all of which should reduce the risk of heart disease." These benefits appear to extend even to those at high risk of heart disease due to diabetes, high blood pressure and previous heart attack.

The mechanisms for alcohol's heart-healthy effects are complex. Now, new research from Europe suggests alcohol is also linked to lower levels of several markers for inflammation, such as C-reactive protein (CRP). Lowering these markers is thought to reduce the risk of heart disease.

*Counterpoint:* Clearly, say experts, drinking three or more alcoholic beverages daily is not healthy; it raises blood pressure, elevates blood triglycerides, increases the risk of stroke and heart failure and contributes to obesity. Moreover, some scientists, like epidemiologist Rod Jackson, Ph.D., from the University of Auckland, suggest the beneficial effects of even moderate alcohol use may be overestimated. In a recent *Lancet* article, he argues that most alcohol studies rely on questionnaires to determine alcohol use, and then track heart disease rates to look for correlations. But such associations can't prove that alcohol is what benefited the heart.

*It's All in Your Head*

*Point:* Several studies suggest that moderate alcohol use lowers the risk of Alzheimer's disease and other forms of dementia. One trial of almost 6,000 volunteers at Boston's Beth Israel Deaconess Medical Center found that, when compared with abstainers, those who had one to six drinks per week had less risk of dementia. And in Harvard's famed Nurses' Health Study, women who drank about one alcoholic beverage daily had half the risk of the most common kind of stroke—from a blocked artery.

*Counterpoint:* There's no question that excessive exposure to alcohol is toxic to the brain. Alcohol abuse accelerates aging of the brain, may cause deficiency of the B vitamin thiamin (which can severely impair cognitive function) and is associated with higher risk of stroke.

*A Diabetes Dilemma*

*Point:* Several large studies have found lower rates of diabetes in people who drink moderately—as much as 36% lower for light-to-moderate drinkers in a Harvard study of 46,000 men. Light-to-moderate drinking also appears to reduce heart disease risk in those with diabetes.

*Counterpoint:* On the other hand, heavy drinking *increases* the risk of diabetes, perhaps at least partly because it contributes to obesity, a prime risk factor. Heavy drinking also increases the risk of metabolic syndrome (abdominal obesity combined with insulin resistance and high blood pressure, elevated cholesterol or elevated triglycerides), particularly if drinking starts early in life.

*A Connection to Cancer*

*Point:* Like fruits, vegetables and tea, red wine and dark beer contain antioxidants called polyphenols, believed to protect against cell damage that can lead to cancer. Xanthohumol, a potent antioxidant found in hops used to make beer, may have the potential to slow cancer cell growth and enhance cancer fighting enzymes.

*Counterpoint:* You don't need to drink alcohol to get antioxidants; you can get plenty from fruits, vegetables and whole grains. Moreover, excessive intake of any kind of alcohol increases the risk of cancer of the mouth, esophagus, stomach, liver, breast and colon. According to the American Cancer Society, even one drink a day (though probably not occasional social drinking) is enough to raise breast cancer risk slightly.

*A Bone to Pick*

*Point:* Recent research from Tufts University on almost 3,000 adult children of participants in the famed Framingham Heart Study found that increased intake of silicon protected bone density in the hip. Earlier Tufts research found beer to be a significant contributor of dietary silicon. Silicon encourages depositing of calcium and other minerals into bone.

*Counterpoint:* Silicon is found in many foods, notably whole grains and root vegetables; you don't need to drink beer to get it. More important, chronic alcohol abuse actually interferes with bone formation and alters calcium, vitamin D and estrogen metabolism, all of which raise the risk of osteoporosis. Moreover, alcohol-related falls are a major cause of bone fracture.

*Weighing the Consequences*

*Point:* Research has debunked the "beer belly" myth that calories from alcohol migrate to your middle more than other calories. In fact, a recent study from the Mayo Clinic of more than 8,200 adults found that those who had a drink daily were 54% *less* likely than non-drinkers to be obese.

*Counterpoint:* But drink to excess and it will cost you; four or more drinks daily raises your odds of obesity by 46%. Any calories you consume that aren't burned off in activity are stored in your body as fat, so adding alcohol calories is likely to result in weight gain, unless you cut back in food intake or exercise more. A 5-ounce glass of wine or a 12-ounce beer averages about 100 to 150 calories, while some mixed drinks can rack up several hundred calories each. Moreover, when you are drinking in social situations, you are likely also eating—often high-calorie foods.

*The Bottom Line.* Clearly, moderation is the key to deriving any benefits from drinking alcohol. As yet, there is not enough evidence to suggest that anyone who doesn't drink should start drinking for health reasons. Moreover, many people have sound reasons for avoiding alcohol; the list of caveats is long.

---

*Clearly, moderation is the key to deriving any benefits from drinking alcohol.*

---

Certainly, alcohol should not be consumed by anyone engaged in activities that require attention, skill or coordination, such as driving or operating machinery. Nor should anyone drink who has a health condition made worse by alcohol, such as high triglycerides, pancreatitis, liver disease, high blood pressure, heart failure or a personal or family history of alcoholism. If you're taking prescription medication, ask your doctor whether it's safe for you to drink.

The final word is still out on whether the antioxidants present in wine and beer offer significant benefits. For those who do choose to imbibe, most research has failed to establish significant advantages to drinking red wine over white wine, beer or spirits.

---

*For those who do choose to imbibe, most research has failed to establish significant advantages to drinking red wine over white wine, beer or spirits.*

---

*What's "A Drink?"*

Researchers from the University of California at Berkeley recently reported on a study in which participants were asked to pour a serving of beer, wine or spirits. The amounts participants poured varied considerably, but most poured nearly 50% more alcohol than in the standard drink. To avoid a heavy pouring hand, stick to the following guide:

A *"serving" of alcohol*=12 ounces beer *or* 5 ounces wine *or* 1.5 ounces 80-proof spirits *or* 1 ounce 100-proof spirits.

*"Moderate use"*=no more than one serving a day for women, two for men.

# 2

# Alcohol Adversely Affects Adolescents

## National Institute on Alcohol Abuse and Alcoholism

*The National Institute on Alcohol Abuse and Alcoholism (NIAAA) is part of the National Institutes of Health and the U.S. Department of Health and Human Services. NIAAA's mission is to conduct and disseminate research in an effort to reduce alcohol-related problems.*

*Most adolescents who begin drinking alcohol at an early age are unaware of the potential consequences. Adolescents turn to alcohol for various reasons including a family history of alcohol abuse and a desire to take chances. Whatever the reasons, alcohol abuse can lead to a number of health risks, risks that are especially acute for adolescents. Unlike adults, teenage brains and organs are still in the process of developing, and alcohol may inhibit the maturity of memory skills, muscles, and bones. Because of the potential harm, prevention and intervention programs are an important element in controlling adolescent alcohol abuse. Raising the minimum drinking age to 21, for instance, has effectively reduced alcohol-related automobile accidents, while programs like Project Northland have successfully deterred alcohol use.*

A lcohol is the drug of choice among youth. Many young people are experiencing the consequences of drinking too much, at too early an age. As a result, underage drinking is a leading public health problem in this country.

National Institute on Alcohol Abuse and Alcoholism, "Underage Drinking," *Alcohol Alert*, January 2006, pp. 1–8. Reproduced by permission.

Each year, approximately 5,000 young people under the age of 21 die as a result of underage drinking; this includes about 1,900 deaths from motor vehicle crashes, 1,600 as a result of homicides, 300 from suicide, as well as hundreds from other injuries such as falls, burns, and drownings.

---

*Research shows the brain keeps developing well into the twenties, during which time it continues to establish important communication connections and further refines its function.*

---

Yet drinking continues to be widespread among adolescents, as shown by nationwide surveys as well as studies in smaller populations. According to data from the 2005 Monitoring the Future (MTF) study, an annual survey of U.S. youth, three-fourths of 12th graders, more than two-thirds of 10th graders, and about two in every five 8th graders have consumed alcohol. And when youth drink they tend to drink intensively, often consuming four to five drinks at one time. MTF data show that 11 percent of 8th graders, 22 percent of 10th graders, and 29 percent of 12th graders had engaged in heavy episodic (or "binge*") drinking within the past two weeks. . .

(*The National Institute on Alcohol Abuse and Alcoholism [NIAAA] defines binge drinking as a pattern of drinking alcohol that brings blood alcohol concentration [BAC] to 0.08 grams percent or above. For the typical adult, this pattern corresponds to consuming five or more drinks [men], or four or more drinks [women], in about 2 hours.)

Research also shows that many adolescents start to drink at very young ages. In 2003, the average age of first use of alcohol was about 14, compared to about 17 [frac12] in 1965. People who reported starting to drink before the age of 15 were four times more likely to also report meeting the criteria for alcohol dependence at some point in their lives. In fact, new research shows that the serious drinking problems (including what is called alcoholism) typically associated with middle age actually begin to appear much earlier, during young adulthood and even adolescence.

Other research shows that the younger children and adolescents are when they start to drink, the more likely they will be to engage in behaviors that harm themselves and others. For example, frequent binge drinkers (nearly 1 million high school students nationwide) are more likely to engage in risky behaviors, including using other drugs such as marijuana and cocaine, having sex with six or more partners, and earning grades that are mostly Ds and Fs in school.

## Why Do Some Adolescents Drink?

As children move from adolescence to young adulthood, they encounter dramatic physical, emotional, and lifestyle changes. Developmental transitions, such as puberty and increasing independence, have been associated with alcohol use. So in a sense, just being an adolescent may be a key risk factor not only for starting to drink but also for drinking dangerously.

*Risk-Taking*—Research shows the brain keeps developing well into the twenties, during which time it continues to establish important communication connections and further refines its function. Scientists believe that this lengthy developmental period may help explain some of the behavior which is characteristic of adolescence—such as their propensity to seek out new and potentially dangerous situations. For some teens, thrill-seeking might include experimenting with alcohol. Developmental changes also offer a possible physiological explanation for why teens act so impulsively, often not recognizing that their actions—such as drinking—have consequences.

*Expectancies*—How people view alcohol and its effects also influences their drinking behavior, including whether they begin to drink and how much. An adolescent who expects drinking to be a pleasurable experience is more likely to drink than one who does not. An important area of alcohol research is focusing on how expectancy influences drinking patterns from childhood through adolescence and into young adulthood. Beliefs about alcohol are established very early in life, even before the child begins elementary school. Before age 9, children generally view alcohol negatively and see drinking as bad, with adverse effects. By about age 13, however, their expectancies shift, becoming more positive. As would be expected, adolescents who drink the most also place the greatest emphasis on the positive and arousing effects of alcohol.

*Sensitivity and Tolerance to Alcohol*—Differences between the adult brain and the brain of the maturing adolescent also may help to explain why many young drinkers are able to consume much larger amounts of alcohol than adults before experiencing the negative consequences of drinking, such as drowsiness, lack of coordination, and withdrawal/hangover effects. This unusual tolerance may help to explain the high rates of binge drinking among young adults. At the same time, adolescents appear to be particularly sensitive to the positive effects of drinking, such as feeling more at ease in social situations, and young people may drink more than adults because of these positive social experiences.

*Personality Characteristics and Psychiatric Comorbidity*—Children who begin to drink at a very early age (before age 12) often share similar personality characteristics that may make them more likely to start drinking. Young people who are disruptive, hyperactive, and aggressive—often referred to as having conduct problems or being antisocial—as well as those who are depressed, withdrawn, or anxious, may be at greatest risk for alcohol problems. Other behavior problems associated with alcohol use include rebelliousness, difficulty avoiding harm or harmful situations, and a host of other traits seen in young people who act out without regard for rules or the feelings of others (i.e., disinhibition).

# Heredity and Environment

*Hereditary Factors*—Some of the behavioral and physiological factors that converge to increase or decrease a person's risk for alcohol problems, including tolerance to alcohol's effects, may be directly linked to genetics. For example, being a child of an alcoholic or having several alcoholic family members places a person at greater risk for alcohol problems. Children of alcoholics (COAs) are between 4 and 10 times more likely to become alcoholics themselves than are children who have no close relatives with alcoholism. COAs also are more likely to begin drinking at a young age and to progress to drinking problems more quickly.

Research shows that COAs may have subtle brain differences which could be markers for developing later alcohol problems. For example, using high-tech brain-imaging techniques, scientists have found that COAs have a distinctive feature in one brainwave pattern (called a P300 response) that could be a marker for later alcoholism risk. Researchers also are investigating other brainwave differences in COAs that may be present long before they begin to drink, including brainwave activity recorded during sleep as well as changes in brain structure and function.

Some studies suggest that these brain differences may be particularly evident in people who also have certain behavioral traits, such as signs of conduct disorder, antisocial personality disorder, sensation-seeking, or poor impulse control. Studying how the brain's structure and function translates to behavior will help researchers to better understand how pre-drinking risk factors shape later alcohol use. For example, does a person who is depressed drink to alleviate his or her depression, or does drinking lead to changes in his brain that result in feelings of depression?

Other hereditary factors likely will become evident as scientists work to identify the actual genes involved in addiction. By analyzing the genetic makeup of people and families with alcohol dependence, researchers have found specific regions on chromosomes that correlate with a risk for alcoholism. Candidate genes for alcoholism risk also have been associated with those regions. The goal now is to further refine regions for which a specific gene has not yet been identified and then determine how those genes interact with other genes and gene products as well as with the environment to result in alcohol dependence. Further research also should shed light on the extent to which the same or different genes contribute to alcohol problems, both in adults and in adolescents.

*Environmental Aspects*—Pinpointing a genetic contribution will not tell the whole story, however, as drinking behavior reflects a complex interplay between inherited and environmental factors, the implications of which are only beginning to be explored in adolescents. And what influences drinking at one age may not have the same impact at another. As Rose [R.J. Rose, researcher] and colleagues show, genetic factors appear to have more influence on adolescent drinking behavior in late adolescence than in mid-adolescence.

---

*Whatever it is that leads adolescents to begin drinking, once they start they face a number of potential health risks.*

---

Environmental factors, such as the influence of parents and peers, also play a role in alcohol use. For example, parents who drink more and who view drinking favorably may have children who drink more, and an adolescent girl with an older or adult boyfriend is more likely to use alcohol and other drugs and to engage in delinquent behaviors.

Researchers are examining other environmental influences as well, such as the impact of the media. Today alcohol is widely available and aggressively promoted through television, radio, billboards, and the Internet. Researchers are studying how young people react to these advertisements. In a study of

3rd, 6th, and 9th graders, those who found alcohol ads desirable were more likely to view drinking positively and to want to purchase products with alcohol logos. Research is mixed, however, on whether these positive views of alcohol actually lead to underage drinking.

## What Are the Health Risks?

Whatever it is that leads adolescents to begin drinking, once they start they face a number of potential health risks. Although the severe health problems associated with harmful alcohol use are not as common in adolescents as they are in adults, studies show that young people who drink heavily may put themselves at risk for a range of potential health problems.

*Brain Effects*—Scientists currently are examining just how alcohol affects the developing brain, but it's a difficult task. Subtle changes in the brain may be difficult to detect but still have a significant impact on long-term thinking and memory skills. Add to this the fact that adolescent brains are still maturing, and the study of alcohol's effects becomes even more complex. Research has shown that animals fed alcohol during this critical developmental stage continue to show long-lasting impairment from alcohol as they age. It's simply not known how alcohol will affect the long-term memory and learning skills of people who began drinking heavily as adolescents.

*Liver Effects*—Elevated liver enzymes, indicating some degree of liver damage, have been found in some adolescents who drink alcohol. Young drinkers who are overweight or obese showed elevated liver enzymes even with only moderate levels of drinking.

*Growth and Endocrine Effects*—In both males and females, puberty is a period associated with marked hormonal changes, including increases in the sex hormones, estrogen and testosterone. These hormones, in turn, increase production of other hormones and growth factors, which are vital for normal organ development. Drinking alcohol during this period of rapid growth and development (i.e., prior to or during puberty) may upset the critical hormonal balance necessary for normal development of organs, muscles, and bones. Studies in animals also show that consuming alcohol during puberty adversely affects the maturation of the reproductive system.

## Preventing Underage Drinking

Complex behaviors, such as the decision to begin drinking or to continue using alcohol, are the result of a dynamic interplay between genes and environment. For example, biological and physiological changes that occur during adolescence may promote risk-taking behavior, leading to early experimentation with alcohol. This behavior then shapes the child's environment, as he or she chooses friends and situations that support further drinking. Continued drinking may lead to physiological reactions, such as depression or anxiety disorders, triggering even greater alcohol use or dependence. In this way, youthful patterns of alcohol use can mark the start of a developmental pathway that may lead to abuse and dependence. Then again, not all young people who travel this pathway experience the same outcomes.

Perhaps the best way to understand and prevent underage alcohol use is to view drinking as it relates to development. This "whole system" approach to underage drinking takes into account a particular adolescent's unique risk and protective factors—from genetics and personality characteristics to social and environmental factors. Viewed in this way, development includes not only the adolescent's inherent risk and resilience but also the current conditions that help to shape his or her behavior.

Children mature at different rates. Developmental research takes this into account, recognizing that during adolescence there are periods of rapid growth and reorganization, alternating with periods of slower growth and integration of body systems. Periods of rapid transitions, when social or cultural factors most strongly influence the biology and behavior of the adolescent, may be the best time to target delivery of interventions. Interventions that focus on these critical development periods could alter the life course of the child, perhaps placing him or her on a path to avoid problems with alcohol.

To date, researchers have been unable to identify a single track that predicts the course of alcohol use for all or even most young people. Instead, findings provide strong evidence for wide developmental variation in drinking patterns within this special population.

## Interventions for Preventing Underage Drinking

Intervention approaches typically fall into two distinct categories: (1) environmental-level interventions, which seek to reduce opportunities for underage drinking, increase penalties for violating minimum legal drinking age (MLDA) and other alcohol use laws, and reduce community tolerance for alcohol use by youth; and (2) individual-level interventions, which seek to change knowledge, expectancies, attitudes, intentions, motivation, and skills so that youth are better able to resist the pro-drinking influences and opportunities that surround them.

Environmental approaches include:

*Raising the Price of Alcohol*—A substantial body of research has shown that higher prices or taxes on alcoholic beverages are associated with lower levels of alcohol consumption and alcohol-related problems, especially in young people.

*Increasing the Minimum Legal Drinking Age*—Today all states have set the minimum legal drinking at age 21. Increasing the age at which people can legally purchase and drink alcohol has been the most successful intervention to date in reducing drinking and alcohol-related crashes among people under age 21. NHTSA [National Highway Traffic Safety Administration] estimates that a legal drinking age of 21 saves 700 to 1,000 lives annually. Since 1976, these laws have prevented more than 21,000 traffic deaths. Just how much the legal drinking age relates to drinking-related crashes is shown by a recent study in New Zealand. Six years ago that country lowered its minimum legal drinking age to 18. Since then, alcohol-related crashes have risen 12 percent among 18- to 19-year-olds and 14 percent among 15- to 17-year-olds. Clearly a higher minimum drinking age can help to reduce crashes and save lives, especially in very young drivers.

*Enacting Zero-Tolerance Laws*—All states have zero-tolerance laws that make it illegal for people under age 21 to drive after any drinking. When the first eight states to adopt zero-tolerance laws were compared with nearby states without such laws, the zero-tolerance states showed a 21-percent greater decline in the proportion of single-vehicle night-time fatal crashes involving drivers under 21, the type of crash most likely to involve alcohol.

*Stepping up Enforcement of Laws*—Despite their demonstrated benefits, legal drinking age and zero-tolerance laws generally have not been vigorously enforced. Alcohol purchase laws aimed at sellers and buyers also can be effective, but resources must be made available for enforcing these laws.

Individual-focused interventions include:

*School-Based Prevention Programs*—The first school-based prevention programs were primarily informational and often used scare tactics; it was assumed that if youth understood the dangers of alcohol use, they would choose not to drink. These programs were ineffective. Today, better programs are available and often have a number of elements in common: They follow social influence models and include setting norms, addressing social pressures to drink, and teaching resistanceskills. These programs also offer interactive and developmentally appropriate information, include peer-led components, and provide teacher training.

*Family-Based Prevention Programs*—Parents' ability to influence whether their children drink is well documented and is consistent across racial/ethnic groups. Setting clear rules against drinking, consistently enforcing those rules, and monitoring the child's behavior all help to reduce the likelihood of underage drinking. The Iowa Strengthening Families Program (ISFP), delivered when students were in grade 6, is a program that has shown long-lasting preventive effects on alcohol use.

## Selected Programs Showing Promise

Environmental interventions are among the recommendations included in the recent National Research Council (NRC) and Institute of Medicine (IOM) report on underage drinking. These interventions are intended to reduce commercial and social availability of alcohol and/or reduce driving while intoxicated. They use a variety of strategies, including server training and compliance checks in places that sell alcohol; deterring adults from purchasing alcohol for minors or providing alcohol to minors; restricting drinking in public places and preventing underage drinking parties; enforcing penalties for the use of false IDs, driving while intoxicated, and violating zero-tolerance laws; and raising public awareness of policies and sanctions.

The following community trials show how environmental strategies can be useful in reducing underage drinking and related problems.

*The Massachusetts Saving Lives Program*—This intervention was designed to reduce alcohol-impaired driving and related traffic deaths. Strategies included the use of drunk-driving checkpoints, speeding and drunk-driving awareness days, speed-watch telephone hotlines, high school peer-led education, and college prevention programs. The 5-year program decreased fatal crashes, particularly alcohol-related fatal crashes involving drivers ages 15–25, and reduced the proportion of 16- to 19-year-olds who reported driving after drinking, in comparison with the rest of Massachusetts. It also made teens more aware of penalties for drunk driving and for speeding.

*The Community Prevention Trial Program*—This program was designed to reduce alcohol-involved injuries and death. One component sought to reduce alcohol sales to minors by enforcing underage sales laws; training sales clerks, owners, and managers to prevent sales of alcohol to minors; and using the media to raise community awareness of underage drinking. Sales to apparent minors (people of legal drinking age who appear younger than age 21) were significantly reduced in the intervention communities compared with control sites.

*Communities Mobilizing for Change on Alcohol*—This intervention, designed to reduce the accessibility of alcoholic beverages to people under age 21, centered on policy changes among local institutions to make underage drinking less acceptable within the community. Alcohol sales to minors were reduced: 18- to 20-year-olds were less likely to try to purchase alcohol or provide it to younger teens, and the number of DUI arrests declined among 18- to 20-year-olds.

*Multicomponent Comprehensive Interventions*—Perhaps the strongest approach for preventing underage drinking involves the coordinated effort of all the elements that influence a child's life—including family, schools, and community. Ideally, intervention programs also should integrate treatment for youth who are alcohol dependent. Project Northland is an example of a comprehensive program that has been extensively evaluated.

Project Northland was tested in 22 school districts in northeastern Minnesota. The intervention included (1) school curricula, (2) peer leadership, (3) parental involvement programs, and (4) communitywide task force activities to address larger community norms and alcohol availability. It targeted adolescents in grades 6 through 12.

Intervention and comparison communities differed significantly in "tendency to use alcohol," a composite measure that combined items about intentions to use alcohol and actual use, as well as in the likelihood of drinking "five or more in a row." Underage drinking was less prevalent in the intervention communities during phase 1; higher during the interim period (suggesting a "catch-up" effect while intervention activities were minimal); and again lower during phase 2, when intervention activities resumed.

Project Northland has been designated a model program by the Substance Abuse and Mental Health Services Administration (SAMHSA), and its materials have been adapted for a general audience. It now is being replicated in ethnically diverse urban neighborhoods.

Today, alcohol is widely available and aggressively promoted throughout society. And alcohol use continues to be regarded, by many people, as a normal part of growing up. Yet underage drinking is dangerous, not only for the drinker but also for society, as is evident by the number of alcohol-involved motor vehicle crashes, homicides, suicides, and other injuries.

People who begin drinking early in life run the risk of developing serious alcohol problems, including alcoholism, later in life. They also are at greater risk for a variety of adverse consequences, including risky sexual activity and poor performance in school.

Identifying adolescents at greatest risk can help stop problems before they develop. And innovative, comprehensive approaches to prevention, such as Project Northland, are showing success in reducing experimentation with alcohol as well as the problems that accompany alcohol use by young people.

# 3

# College Campuses Should Regulate Alcohol Abuse

*Paul Gruenewald and Robert Saltz*

*Paul Gruenewald is a scientific director and Robert Saltz is a senior research scientist at the Prevention Research Center of the Pacific Institute for Research and Evaluation in Berkeley, California.*

*Alcohol abuse on college campuses is responsible for homicides, fatal accidents, rapes, and automobile collisions. Colleges have attempted to educate students on the dangers of alcohol abuse but these measures have fallen short. Instead, colleges need to instigate a series of controls designed to limit the access to alcohol on college campuses, including employee training at establishments selling alcohol, stricter drunk-driving enforcement, and limiting alcohol licenses for new businesses.*

Reports of alcohol-related mayhem and tragedies are piling up once again on college campuses. In October [2004] it was the Harvard University student convicted of manslaughter for stabbing a restaurant worker in a fight following a night of drinking, and two Marshall University football players accused of assaulting a woman in a bar. A University of Delaware student who was struck and killed by a train on her way home from a fraternity party had a blood alcohol concentration three times the legal limit. A Colorado State University student was found dead Saturday [December 11, 2004] in an ap-

Paul Gruenewald and Robert Saltz, "College Drinking Is Not a Given," *Christian Science Monitor*, December 14, 2004. Copyright © 2004, The Christian Science Monitor. All rights reserved. Reproduced by permission.

parent alcohol-related incident. CSU recently formed a task force on drinking after another student's death in September [2004]. Police said the 19-year-old woman had consumed some 40 beers that evening.

But these high-profile incidents are only part of the story. For every tragedy or event that makes the news, there are hundreds of thousands of other alcohol-related problems on campuses that nobody hears about. The National Institute on Alcohol Abuse and Alcoholism estimates that each year, drinking by college students has resulted in 1,400 deaths (usually from drinking and driving), 500,000 injuries, 600,000 assaults, and 70,000 sexual assaults or date rapes. Alcohol-fueled riots at Halloween and following sports victories are almost regular occurrences. The solution is to change the overall drinking environment that envelops collegiate life in America and provides fertile ground for these problems.

For years, colleges have relied on educating young people about responsible behavior and the dangers of alcohol, though at the same time alcohol remained easily available, attractive, and inexpensive for students. An alcohol information pamphlet handed out at freshman orientation cannot compete with "Nickel Beer Nite" at a pub across the street from the dorms or free beer at a rowdy fraternity party. If we want college kids to behave responsibly, we need to build the environment to support them in making the right decisions.

Colleges tend to make the mistake of searching for one easy solution or tactic, such as an alcohol awareness campaign. Instead, they should think about preventing college drinking the same way we prevent traffic accidents—with an array of protective measures: seat belts, air bags, traffic lights, speed limits, and police enforcement. What most colleges do is akin to asking young adults to drive responsibly, then sending them out on a highway with no speed limit.

## Controlling Alcohol on Campus

Most people, particularly college kids themselves, say that students are going to drink a lot no matter what. Far from being a statement of fact, however, this belief reflects the popular acceptance of the heavy-drinking environment around so many college campuses. But that environment can be changed through a multifaceted program of controls on the sale, service, and promotion of alcohol.

This does work. In 1998, the Prevention Research Center completed five years of community trials to reduce alcohol abuse, both adult and underage, in Oceanside and Salinas, Calif., and in Florence, S.C.

A collection of control measures were enacted, such as training employees at bars and liquor stores not to sell alcohol to people who were obviously intoxicated or underage; increasing drunk-driving enforcement by police; controlling the density of bars and liquor stores by limiting new licenses, not reissuing licenses for locations that went out of business, and closing down repeat violators of liquor laws; and mobilizing community groups to support these efforts.

---

*A protective system of alcohol controls can change the long-established drinking environment of American colleges and universities. . . .*

---

The measures contributed to a 43 percent reduction in assault injuries reported at emergency rooms and a 10 percent drop in nighttime traffic crashes causing injury. Surveys also showed a 49 percent decline in people reporting heavy drinking.

This same approach can work for college campuses. A recent study by the Harvard School of Public Health showed positive results for five campuses that made serious efforts to control alcohol. And last year's landmark study by the National Academy of Sciences on how to reduce underage drinking endorsed similar alcohol-control measures to change the drinking environment that leads to youth alcohol abuse. Additional controls recommended for colleges include halting drink specials at bars near campus, expanding substance-free residence halls, promoting alcohol-free activities on campus, coordinating campus and city police to crack down on rowdy house parties, and requiring registration for beer kegs so police can track who's responsible if problems result.

While there is no way to know when or where the next tragedy will occur, the larger impacts of college drinking affect nearly every campus on an almost daily basis. A protective system of alcohol controls can change the long-established drinking environment at American colleges and universities and thereby reduce alcohol-related deaths, as well as the less publicized problems of assaults, injuries, rapes, and property damage.

# 4

# Alcohol Abuse Harms Adolescent Development

## Nutrition Health Review

Nutrition Health Review *provides health and medical information to communities, residents, and professionals.*

*Alcohol is both mentally and physically addicting, and long-term alcohol abuse can cause permanent brain damage. Alcohol abuse can likewise lead to liver and pancreatic disease. If a person abuses alcohol for extended periods of time, she or he may become addicted; when an addicted person attempts to refrain from alcohol, she or he will suffer withdrawal symptoms. Even if an alcohol abuser successfully withdraws, she or he will remain sensitized to the effects of alcohol. Withdrawal from alcohol is a serious matter, and may be dangerous without proper medical supervision. Alcohol abuse may lead to violent behavior in certain personality types, and, over time, memory loss. As with brain damage, extensive alcohol abuse may cause irreparable damage to the body's organs. Alcohol abuse is even more dangerous to pregnant women, their fetuses, and the developing brain of a child or teenager.*

[N*utritian Health Review] Is the addiction to alcohol physical or mental?*

[William Schoemaker, PhD] Both. There are physical symptoms when people who chronically consume alcohol withdraw from it, and there is also a psychological dependence on alcohol. So it is both.

*Can people who experience the physical addiction also have the mental addiction, or are these both mutually exclusive?*

They usually go together.

*Is there a difference in the brain chemistry of a long-time alcoholic and a nondrinker?*

When someone has been an alcoholic for a long time, many of the cells in the brain die; as a result, their brain is going to be different. If you looked at the constituents of the brain, you would see that certain cell populations have dropped out—disappeared—in the alcoholics.

And if you do a CT [computed tomography] or PET [positron emission tomography] scan on these people, the total volume of brain is smaller. There has been some shrinkage; the shrinkage is due to death of cells that are not replaced.

*If an alcoholic stops drinking, does the brain return to its healthy size or does it remain shrunken?*

Well, if it has gotten to the point where the cells have died, they do not come back. If it has gone to that extent, then ceasing to drink is going to stop the neurodegenerative trend, but it is not going to go back to normal. Certainly, there are many people like this, and they can live happy and useful lives, even with a certain amount of brain damage.

*What kind of problems come about from a long-term change in the brain?*

Many things change. The lesions from long-term alcohol use have a certain pattern. Many of the people who are in this situation are found to have Korsakoff's disease. Motor impairment and cerebellum impairment develop, so balance is affected. Memory and cognitive function are affected.

Many times people cannot take care of themselves, and they may need to be hospitalized or placed in nursing homes.

*Do brain cells regenerate once they are gone?*

No.

*Does alcohol abuse have any effect on a person's physical appearance?*

You really can't tell by looking at people whether they are addicted. Certain vascular conditions can show. This sometimes happens with alcoholics, especially, in the nasal area. Sometimes you'll see this, but there are other things that cause this vasculitis, not just alcohol. You will see it in long-term alcoholics. You have to do a medical work-up and a psychiatric workup, with an emphasis on questions about substance abuse to determine whether a person has alcoholism.

Certainly, other kinds of chemical addictions, say cocaine or heroin addiction, in which the time course to reach the addiction state is much shorter, you can't tell by looking; there are no physical findings at all.

*What diseases or physical problems can come about from alcohol addiction?*

Many, many things. Chronic alcoholism is related to liver disease and cirrhosis, which can be fatal. Pancreatic disease also can be life-threatening. People may also have cardiovascular complications. It is a number of different things.

## Alcohol and the Brain

*If you take a drink, what happens in the brain?*

If it were easy to tell you this in "1, 2, 3," we wouldn't be studying it so intensely. But this gets technical.

Alcohol has effects on different neurotransmitter systems in the brain. In low amounts, it affects the GABA [gamma amino butyric acid] system. As the blood levels become higher, alcohol affects another common transmitter system, NMDA glutamate. This is a description of an acute alcohol effect, such as what happens if you go out drinking on a Friday night. These effects can be seen and felt. The next day, depending on how much you drink, the system would reset itself and it would be back to normal.

With chronic alcohol use, the cells in the brain and other tissue now find themselves maintained in a fluid that contains alcohol and they adapt to it. These adaptations have to do with neurotransmission in the brain and with the brain protecting itself from too much excitement or too much inhibition. You can see this when someone who has been consuming alcohol for a long time withdraws from it. Now, those cells have made these adaptations to an environment with a lot of alcohol, but now the alcohol is gone. Those cells are not prepared and not adapted for an environment that does not contain alcohol. That is what causes withdrawal symptoms, and it takes several days to a week for them to go back to where they were before, in a certain way, and not misfiring or pathologically reacting.

*Do they ever go all the way back, or is there always some kind of damage?*

It's hard to know on a cellular basis, but we know on the organism basis. People who have had long-term alcoholism and then managed to stop drinking are probably not going back to where they were before. They are changed somewhat, and they are much more sensitive to alcohol. It is a process we call "sensitization," and it happens with other psychotropic drugs as well.

Now, they can be sober for quite a long time—many years. If they then take a drink after all those years, it's not like they were just starting off as a teenager. They have the syndrome of craving and the syndrome of out-of-control drinking, and those reinstate themselves very rapidly. These patients are very sensitive to alcohol, and they are out of control very quickly.

If you know anything about Alcoholics Anonymous (AA), these facts are understood from the very beginning. When people from AA introduce themselves, they say 'Hi, my name is Joe, and I'm an alcoholic,' even if they haven't had a drink in 30 years. They somehow understand that they are different and that they have to continue to work to stay sober because there is probably some irreversible change that has gone on.

These people are recovered in terms that they are not drinking, and they can lead a pretty normal life; however, it is never back to ground zero. They must always be careful. Many of them understand this and continue to go to AA meetings for their whole life. They feel that they need that support and that they are not how they were when they started.

*What is the difference between craving and an addiction?*

That's a good question, actually. A "craving" is a subjective feeling of want or desire. A craving can be for anything. You can have a craving for candy bars or a glass of orange juice, but we don't consider you addicted to those.

---

*Withdrawing from long-term alcohol use is a serious medical problem and it should be supervised medically.*

---

An addiction has to do with chemical substances that have a profound effect on the brain. The [substance] takes over a person's life. The thoughts and actions of addicted persons are directed toward obtaining a drug or getting another drink, even though the world around them is crumbling. Cravings are just normal, everyday feelings, but they can also be for these drugs.

## Alcohol and Withdrawal

*How can we explain someone who can drink heavily for an extended period of time and then give it up abruptly?*

I don't think that there is such a person. If people are drinking every day for a long period of time, they can't quit suddenly. The body is in this neuroadapted state. The whole nervous system is going to scream out.

In fact, people shouldn't try to do that. Withdrawing from long-term alcohol use is a serious medical problem and it should be supervised medically. There are medications that people can take that ease this transition with the knowledge we have of what goes on with the cells. They can ease transition and make it less risky. The withdrawal process can be life-threatening. In the old days, before this was understood, many people died trying to withdraw from alcohol.

*How would they die?*

If addicts were unable to obtain the substance, they went into withdrawal. Withdrawal can be very severe, and it affects the entire nervous system. It is not clear exactly why addicts might have died, although it is suggested that their sympathetic nervous system is highly activated in that condition, which might have affected the heart rate and the vascular system. In addition, the condition of the brain cells might be related to the occurrence of convulsions, so that's also serious. They can have an epilepsy-like fit—uncontrolled convulsions.

*Are drugs available to treat withdrawal symptoms?*

Oh yes.

*How do they treat them?*

I mentioned that alcohol affects the GABA system. A class of drugs called benzodiazepines act on GABA receptors by keeping the GABA receptor from getting too wild; these agents can then be tapered slowly. Sometimes an anti-convulsant called carbamazepine is also used. Chronic alcoholics may also have nutritional and metabolic deficiencies, and these problems must be treated as well. Alcoholics are almost always thiamine-deficient. Levels of niacin and folate, together with blood electrolytes, must be monitored. Other drugs might be given to control autonomic hyperactivity, which occurs during withdrawal. Finally, these patients should be under medical supervision.

*Do the relapse rates for people who are addicted to drugs like nicotine . . . differ from the rates for alcoholics?*

Well, everything is different. One of the most addicting drugs is cocaine, and yet cocaine withdrawal is not associated with dangerous physical withdrawal symptoms, except for psychiatric symptoms, including depression, which can lead to suicide. Nicotine is one of the most severe addictions that people have; this substance is more addicting than alcohol.

Nicotine withdrawal creates some symptoms, but they are not as severe and usually people can handle it. People can buy nicotine gum or nicotine patches, so withdrawal from nicotine doesn't have the same physiological effect as alcohol withdrawal. Heroin withdrawal and addiction probably should be managed because there are uncomfortable and painful consequences. But none of them are as life-threatening as those of alcohol withdrawal.

*In movies, sometimes people treat withdrawal by locking themselves in a room, or a person is sedated until the symptoms go away. Is there any merit to these methods?*

I don't think you should sedate people for as long as that, because withdrawal might take several days or weeks. They can be given other kinds of support—psychological support. That's what these detoxification centers can try to do. Everyone else there is trying to accomplish the same thing, so you have group support.

That kind of Hollywood view of withdrawal, where the person is just okay, isn't exactly true. First, we mentioned that when people "come down" from an addiction to go clean, they are not the same as when they started. They have to be careful. Second, one of the things that will happen—especially in the time period close to when they withdraw—is that they will have a very strong craving and will be very susceptible to trying to go back to re-experience the feelings that they had when they first started using the drugs.

## Alcohol and Brain Impairment

*Does the brain of a person who craves alcohol differ from that of an alcoholic?*

They are starting to use MRI [Magnetic Resonance Imaging] scans for this. But it is unlikely that MRI would become routine for this purpose; it is a tool for research. You can't see either addiction or craving by looking at the brain. If a person has been consuming alcohol for a long time, the brain cells start to die. You can tell that by using brain scans when the craving reaches a moderately severe level. But craving itself is not going to show up in a way that you can view it.

*Why does alcohol cause violent behavior?*

In low doses, there is a release of behavioral inhibition, and that is why it's such a popular drink. People who are socially uninhibited become more friendly and outgoing after a drink or two. But for some people, the inhibition may be necessary to keep other kinds of feelings from coming out. So when they drink, now you're seeing a different kind of person, one who might be prone to violence.

It is not just the alcohol. It is the combination of the alcohol with some kind of underlying personality structure.

*How does alcohol result in memory loss and motor impairment?*

The long-term effects cause cell death. Some of those cells are related to memory, and some are related to motor impairment. For instance, in a temporary, one-night-of-drinking situation, a lot of people wake up the next day and cannot remember what happened. That is because alcohol, in higher doses, affects the NMDA glutamate system, which must operate correctly for memories to be incorporated. When people drink to excess, that system just stops working. The drinker loses the memory of what happened during that time.

Of course, too much alcohol can cause people to become sedated and to pass out; in such a situation, of course, they will not remember any of that.

*Some say that blackouts are a sure sign that you have a drinking problem. Is it possible to black out with occasional use and not be an alcoholic?*

I suppose. A so-called binge-drinker might drink to excess on the weekends and might have blackouts. However, it is difficult to know where excessive binge-drinking ends and the start of more addictive drinking begins. The binges sometimes start on a Friday night and end on a Monday morning, but then maybe a person will want to get a head start on the weekend and start earlier. When you get to that point, you're in the realm of becoming an alcoholic.

*How does alcohol raise the risk of stroke?*

We mentioned that alcohol has cardiovascular effects. The blood vessels are highly innervated by sympathetic and parasympathetic and other aspects of the nervous system. As alcohol takes its toll on the nervous system, some suggest that the plasticity and the elasticity of the blood vessels start to decrease. This event would contribute to a cerebrovascular accident.

Alcohol does many things to many organ systems. Alcohol affects the liver, which makes a lot of substances and chemicals that the brain and the rest of the body need. Now you're cutting down on those, and perhaps the ratio of substances in the blood stream is changed in alcoholics. This may contribute to the building up of plaques and occlusions in the blood vessels.

*How much abuse can the liver take before the damage is irreversible?*

Well, the abuse is not measured; we just treat the patient. The liver is tested to see how serious the disease is and to try to reverse it. There are other causes of liver disease, of course, but I would say that next to the brain, the liver is very complicated and very vital. If you don't take care of it, you will pay a price. Even small amounts of dysfunction will be felt. The liver has certain regenerative properties. If you can get it treated in time, it is likely to recuperate.

*What effect does alcohol have on an unborn child in a mother who might not know that she is pregnant?*

This is a real problem. Sometimes mothers did not know that they were pregnant; they were drinking regularly, then found out they were pregnant, stopped drinking, and still had a child who had growth retardation, small brain size, mild to moderate retardation—all signs of fetal alcohol syndrome.

So, heavy drinking at any time during pregnancy can be a problem. The effects vary in different periods of pregnancy when the alcohol is present. In most women who give birth to a child with fetal alcohol syndrome, the mothers have been drinking all the time. Embryonic development is highly regulated, and excess alcohol abuse can upset that regulation.

*What kind of damage can alcohol do to the developing brain of a child or teenager?*

We are trying to learn the answer to this now. We learn about these things using animal models. There haven't been too many attempts to look at an animal model of teenagers. When researchers examine juveniles, they find that alcohol can be quite damaging. I don't know if the effects would be any different in adults, but the systems of younger people seem to be more sensitive. Usually, individuals in that age range will sample alcohol and drink it from time to time, but they are not usually alcoholics. It isn't the same kind of problem as with adults. Adolescence is still a vulnerable time, and since the evidence is that more and more young people are drinking alcohol, we are paying more attention to the consequences of adolescent drinking.

# 5

# Developmental Harm Caused by Alcohol Is Overstated

## John Buell

*John Buell is a columnist for the* Bangor Daily News.

*While experts have warned teens of the dangers of alcohol consumption, the evidence that moderate consumption is dangerous is far from conclusive. Scientists have often drawn conclusions from tests conducted on rats or alcohol-addicted teens, leading, other experts believe, to unrepresentative results. Part of the imbalance stems from funding sources with political motives. Since research relating to alcohol and the brain remains inconclusive, parents should tell teens the truth: some studies conclude that alcohol may cause brain damage, others that it does not.*

Several years ago, I wrote a column suggesting that binge drinking in college would increase if society intensified campaigns against all underage drinking. Recent publicity about new scientific evidence on alcohol and teen brains has given me pause. Nonetheless, conversations with scholars on both sides lead me to conclude that disciplining teenagers for moderate alcohol consumption is neither scientifically justified nor productive.

One should be wary about claims for new scientific discoveries. Findings qualify as discoveries only when results are replicated over time and across cultures. Dr. David J. Hanson, a respected expert on the politics and etiology of alcohol abuse, points out that many "new findings" are extrapolations

John Buell, "Dissenting Ideas on New Teen Brain Science," *Bangor Daily News*, June 13, 2006. Reproduced by permission of the author.

from studies on rats, which often react to drugs in ways different from humans. Others are based on severely alcohol-dependent teens, some as young as 12. Though such studies are cautionary, their applicability to moderate drinking by 16- to 20-year-olds has been contested by many experts.

Earlier attempts to tie cognitive loss to moderate alcohol consumption in adults have been contradicted by later studies that attribute the impairment to educational and cultural deficiencies. In addition, cognition is complex. It is measured in different ways. As with IQ tests, questions reflect cultural predispositions. No small set of findings can be decisive.

In adults, there is also strong evidence that moderate drinking, while slightly increasing the incidence of relatively uncommon hemorrhagic stroke, reduces the risk of more likely ischemic (clot) stroke. Since arterial hardening starts at a very young age, might moderate alcohol consumption convey some long-term cardiovascular benefit? An intriguing but little-reported Australian study suggests cognitive enhancement from moderate alcohol consumption by subjects as young as 20.

## Dissenting Ideas on Teen Brain Science

Unfortunately, over the years scientists working under grants from the National Institute on Alcohol Abuse and Alcoholism have authored studies indicating benefits from moderate consumption among adults only to see some of these studies withheld or under publicized by their political superiors. As in recent cases with marijuana, a researcher today who documented benefits from any stigmatized substance might see the results suppressed and future funding ended.

Even honest brain research confronts an inherent dilemma that makes conclusions problematic. Language, thought and culture—including the culture of "having a drink"—are enabled and affected by the circuitry and neurochemistry of the brain. But by the same token, thought techniques, such as meditation, exert observable effects on the architecture of the brain. In addition, once evolution enables linguistic capacity, distinct languages, cultures and beliefs emerge through social interactions. Culture and biochemistry both matter.

---

*If we withhold alcohol, why not iPods, cell phones or Coca-Cola, which become hard-to-break lifestyle habits that may harm cognitive development?*

---

An individual's beliefs can have a discernible effect on the brain. Neurons that fire together wire together, in the famous phrase. Some studies indicate that alcohol's ability to induce violence is intensified when subjects are instructed on the violence-enhancing propensities of alcohol. Might research subjects informed that even small amounts of alcohol make one stupid not respond in an analogous manner? I don't know the answer, but stigmatizing all underage drinking makes it more difficult to obtain data and affects the outcome of the research.

When I voice these concerns to some public health advocates, they respond that until the science is in, the default position should be to tell our teens not to drink. My default position is to tell teenagers the truth: some scientists see an indication that moderate alcohol intake may damage the brain, but other scientists dispute these conclusions. Some even believe the direction of current research points toward possible benefits from moderate teen consumption. I emphasize the one strong scientific consensus: excessive consumption is dangerous both short and long term.

Finally, even if negative epidemiological studies on teen drinking become much more solid, it does not follow that if parents or police criminalize, punish, or even stigmatize moderate drinking by 16- to 20-year-olds, social benefits will follow. As long as we allow 18-year-olds to vote and join the army, and allow even 16-year-olds to drive, they, like older citizens are already making equally serious risk-reward choices on a daily basis and may resent and rebel against our sanctions.

If we withhold alcohol, why not iPods, cell phones or Coca-Cola, which become hard-to-break lifestyle habits that may harm cognitive development? Teens can and do learn to live with ambiguity. When parents impose absolute restrictions that many of them did not follow and base these norms on controversial or politically motivated science, destructive consequences follow. Respect for law, parents, and public health authorities suffers.

We should discuss all risks with teens. I tell teens and adults—to little avail—that for the vast majority of them, cutting their driving in half would convey far more obvious health benefits to us all than cutting their drinking in half. Our government would do better focusing on our dangerous transportation system and on the inadequate educational and economic opportunities that often lead modest pleasures to become destructive addictions.

# 6

# Alcohol Advertising Has No Effect on Underage Drinking

*Maia Szalavitz*

*Maia Szalavitz is the coauthor, with Dr. Joseph Volpicelli, of* Recovery Options: The Complete Guide: How You and Your Loved Ones Can Understand and Treat Alcohol and Other Drug Problems *and the author of* Help at Any Cost.

*A number of studies have drawn a connection between alcohol advertising and alcohol abuse, but the results are inconclusive, and, in some cases, misleading. Experimental research and survey studies have found little connection between youth alcohol consumption and advertising, though it has been difficult to isolate why this is true. Certain econometric analysis have identified a possible correlation between advertising and drinking, but the results remain inconclusive. Advertising research is a very complex field. People respond to the same ads in different ways; over a span of time, the same person may respond to an ad in different ways. In the end, banning ads in one or two media venues—even if a connection between alcohol advertising and teen drinking can be proved—is likely to prove ineffective because advertisers will increase funding in other venues.*

Every so often, controversy arises over a particular ad that appears to encourage children to drink alcohol. Anti-alcohol advocacy groups—notably the Center on Alcohol Marketing and Youth (CAMY), the National Center on Addiction and Substance Abuse (CASA), and the Center on Alcohol Ad-

Maria Szalavitz, "Alcohol and Advertising," *STATS at George Mason University*, October 21, 2005. Reproduced by permission.

vertising—are often involved in these controversies with reports on what they see as egregious ads or trends.

Probably the best known example was a 1996 survey by the Center on Alcohol Advertising which showed that the Budweiser frogs were recognized by almost as many kids as Bugs Bunny a year after they were introduced. Such findings would appear to bolster calls for a crackdown on the way that alcohol is marketed; yet research on the effects of alcohol advertising on youth has not shown that advertising has much of an impact on teen drinking.

At least, this is the conclusion reached by a number of reviews of evidence, including the 10th Special Report to Congress on Alcohol and Health by the National Institute on Alcohol Abuse and Alcoholism (NIAAA) in June 2000. Nevertheless, the multitude of factors involved in trying to measure the effect of advertising on alcohol consumption makes this a complex and difficult issue to study. Despite the large body of research available, the data is often contradictory and confusing.

In order to know where current research stands and how to make sense of the problem, it is helpful to break down the different types of research as follows. . . .

## Advertising Research

### Experimental Research

The experimental research on exposure to alcohol advertising has found either no effect or a small, short-lasting effect on attitudes towards drinking. However, these experimental studies all share a major flaw: They looked at attitudes towards alcohol following exposure to alcohol advertising (as seen on TV in a reel of other commercials, or in magazines); but they did not measure actual drinking behavior.

Though attitudes towards alcohol and drinking often correlate, this correlation is not absolute. To take an extreme example, an alcoholic may have highly negative attitudes towards alcohol and still drink heavily. Similarly, teenagers may feel inhibited about expressing positive beliefs about drinking, to adults, because it is illegal for people their age. Experimental studies also cannot account for the effects of exposure to thousands of ads in varying media over a lifetime.

A study typical of the research in this area exposed groups of fifth and eighth grade students, who identified themselves as non-drinkers, to one of three conditions. One group saw commercials that included five beer ads; a second group saw commercials that included two anti-drinking public service announcements (PSAs); and a third group saw both the beer ads and the anti-drinking PSAs. The control group saw only soft drink commercials placed among other advertising. Although the students remembered the relevant commercials, neither the beer ads nor the PSAs had any effect on their responses to a survey about the putative positive effects of drinking (i.e., greater social acceptance, success with the opposite sex, etc.).

*Survey Studies*

Surveys in alcohol advertising research typically poll people about their attitudes towards alcohol ads and drinking and then look for connections between such variables. In this body of research, several studies have linked an increased "liking" of alcohol ads to an increased intention to drink.

One study surveyed 500 New Zealanders aged 10–17 about their responses to beer commercials. The more the kids said they liked the ads, the more often they said they intended to drink at age 20. However, the correlation between liking alcohol ads and actual drinking behavior was not great enough to be statistically significant. Other survey research found that the more teens judged as being at high risk for alcohol problems identified with the situations in the alcohol ads, the more likely they were to think positively about drinking.

While the survey research consistently shows that advertising has, at most, a small effect on teen drinking and a greater effect on teen attitudes about drinking, it cannot show cause and effect. As a result, it is hard to know what is really happening. For instance, while advertising may make alcohol attractive to some teens, they could just as easily enjoy or be attracted to alcohol advertising because they already hold positive attitudes towards drinking.

In other words, the fact that teens who like alcohol ads are more likely to want to drink may simply reflect their pre-existing attitudes, rather than show an effect of the commercials. And the fact that the effect on behavior is much smaller than that on attitudes again shows that one cannot rely on attitudes alone to measure the real world effects of ads.

*Econometric Analysis*

Econometric analysis looks at how alcohol advertising affects other alcohol-related variables such as consumption rates, alcohol abuse rates and drunk driving casualties. Most of the research in this area has found that advertising has no effect on such variables.

However, some econometric analyses have found effects: A 1997 study looked at the relationship between automobile fatalities and the amount of alcohol advertising in the top 75 American media markets. It found a correlation between alcohol advertising and both total and nighttime crash deaths (the latter are particularly likely to be alcohol-linked). The study concluded that a total ban on alcohol advertising might save 5,000 to 10,000 lives a year. Since the number of alcohol-related auto fatalities has totaled about 17,000 annually since 1995, according to the National Highway Traffic Safety Administration, and since the study's findings are not consistent with the rest of the literature, such figures probably overestimate the impact of a total advertising ban.

Curiously, this study found that the effect on drunk driving deaths was concentrated among *adults*. Advertising did not seem to affect drunken driving rates among youths. This may be because drunk driving deaths among youths already account for a much smaller proportion of crashes than they do among adults. This may reflect the greater role played by inexperience in crashes caused by young drivers or, possibly, the impact of prevention efforts.

For example education could have already deterred the most easily affected youth and left a core group that is much harder to influence (About 40% of crash deaths caused by adult drivers are alcohol-related; for youths, the proportion is about 20%).

Another econometric analysis that found connections between youth drinking and advertising was published as a working paper for the National Bureau of Economic Research in May 2003. It looked for correlations between data from two major national youth surveys: Monitoring the Future (which samples 63,000 high school students) and The National Longitudinal Survey of Youth Behavior conducted by the Bureau of Labor Statistics, and alcohol advertising in local markets as compiled by Competitive Media Reporting. The data used were from the years 1996–1998. The study concluded that eliminating alcohol advertising completely would reduce the proportion of adolescents who drink each month from 25% to 21%. More significantly, the study claimed that a total ad ban would reduce the population of teen binge drinkers from 12% of adolescents to seven percent.

An international study also supported the idea that advertising restrictions can help. It looked at alcohol abuse in 17 different countries. The research examined the connection between restrictions on TV and radio advertising and both consumption rates and driving fatalities. The study found that alcohol consumption was lowered by 16% and traffic deaths by 10% in countries with the greatest restrictions on TV and radio ads. But this relationship was confounded by the fact that the countries that adopted such advertising restrictions started out with lower rates of alcohol problems and deeper anti-alcohol attitudes among their populations.

And studies of advertising bans carried out in the real world have shown that they have little or no impact on consumption. For example, research on three different provinces of Canada—British Columbia, Manitoba and Saskatchewan—that banned alcohol ads at three different times did not find reductions in drinking. It is possible, however, that these results were contaminated by exposure to alcohol ads on American television, which remained during the Canadian bans.

---

*A parent, for example, may find a frightening anti-alcohol ad effective, while a teenager may find the risks associated with drinking to be part of the thrill.*

---

## The Complexity of Advertising Research

As is clear from the above, drawing conclusions about the effects of alcohol advertising is difficult. Advertising effects are hard to study in general, because there are so many different factors that influence how people respond to ads. There is the problem of saturation; if a high level of advertising already exists, a further increase won't make much difference, and small cutbacks won't have much of an effect either. There is the problem of pulsing—the influence of both advertising and ad saturation decays over time, so short pulses of ads followed by their absence may have more effect than simple increases in the total number of ads. The "pulse" effect can then confound studies that compare total amounts of alcohol advertising to variables like the number of car crashes.

Targeting can also make measurement difficult: CAMY and other groups opposed to alcohol advertising often make much of measures of the proportion of under-21s exposed to alcohol ads compared to adults, saying in several reports that they've found that youth are exposed to more ads than adults. But these measures are controversial for several reasons, not the least of which is that 19- and 20-year olds are legal adults by every other criterion used other than drinking age. It's nearly impossible to target 21-year olds, for example, and not bring in 19- and 20-year olds as well. Most of the "over-exposure" to alcohol ads that activists cite occurs in the intermediate age range—not the group most parents are worried about when they think about under-age drinkers.

Further, some people will be affected by certain ads, while others will respond in the exact opposite way. And the same person may respond differently to the same ad at different times in his or her life, or even according to different moods. A parent, for example, may find a frightening anti-alcohol ad effective, while a teenager may find the risks associated with drinking to be part of the thrill. A teen who has just lost a friend in a drunk-driving accident may respond one way, while a teen who is drunk at a party may respond in another.

Gender, race, culture, and age all matter. The level of repetition matters (some people like an ad at first, then come to hate it; others find that it grows on them over time). Context can be important. Certain media may be more effective for some people, certain messages more effective for others. Fashion trends also make a big difference—specific drinks, like particular drugs, go in and out of style in particular cultures and subcultures. Demand, related to these shifts, can drive advertising just as advertising drives demand. And the mixed messages American culture sends about alcohol and its significance in our rites of passage and celebrations further complicates these studies.

The research is clear, however, that banning advertising in only one or two media—say TV and radio—is ineffective, as advertising will increase in other media to fill the gap. While other media venues may then become saturated with ads, decreasing the effectiveness of each one, the overall media climate returns to a similar level of saturation, as research on bans of tobacco advertising on television and radio have demonstrated.

# 7

# Alcohol Advertising Promotes Underage Drinking

*Nina Riccio*

*Nina Riccio wrote the following article for* Current Health *in 2002.*

*Alcohol advertising consistently displays images that attract a younger audience. Although these companies do spend money on campaigns aimed at diminishing underage drinking, the dollars spent on these efforts are minimal. Because teens who abuse alcohol are more likely to be violent, or drive drunk, we all need to take seriously the issue of advertising to this demographic.*

Jesse, age 20, has been sober for about four years. But when he was drinking heavily, his choice of booze depended on image. "It couldn't be just any brand Bud was OK—it has a cool image. There's another brand that's a lot cheaper but no one would ever bring that to a party. It tastes all right, but the can just looks stupid."

## TV Ads Target a Young Audience

The makers of Budweiser have spent millions of dollars making sure Jesse and others like him think Bud has a "cool" image. In 2000, for example, brewers spent $770 million on TV ads and another $15 million on radio commercials. Add a few hundred million more for promotions and sponsorships.

Nina Riccio, "How Alcohol Ads Target Teens: They're Cute. They're Funny. But Did You Ever Think That Those Funny, Sometimes Annoying Frogs Croaking the Name of a Beer Could Be Dangerous to You?" *Current Health* 2, vol. 29, no. 1, September 2002, pp. 14–17. Reproduced by permission.

Besides the Budweiser frogs, you're probably familiar with a spotted dog named Spuds, lizards, and canines from outer space. The packaging on many of these products is humorous, goofy, and even cartoonish. Some feature college kids on spring break. Most of these manufacturers have their own Websites, where viewers can log on and play games or enter contests to win prizes with insignias on them. Clearly, they're aimed at you, not your parents.

Jesse now understands that he played right into the hands of alcohol manufacturers. "Bud seems particularly shameful because they really play to kids," he says. But they're certainly not the only ones. "Alcopops, like the hard lemonades are aimed at people who don't like the taste of alcohol. They're like soda pop."

---

*Studies show that teens who begin drinking are four times as likely to become alcoholics as those who don't begin drinking until age 21.*

---

## Who's in Charge Here?

The makers of beer, wine coolers, and alcopops deny that they market to teens. In fact, they point out, they spend millions of dollars on public service announcements telling underage kids not to drink. They put up billboards to drinkers to "drink responsibly," or others admonishing them not to drink and drive. They contribute to community groups and give grocers cards with tips on how to spot fake IDs. But the money they spend on these programs is just a small fraction of what's spent on overall advertising. In fact, it's estimated that for each public service message a kid hears about drinking responsibly, he or she is likely to see 25 to 50 ads promoting beer or wine.

The bottom line in business is that the more you advertise, the higher your sales. And studies show that the more they're exposed to beer ads, the more likely teens are to have positive feelings about drinking, and the more likely they will be to drink as adults.

Whether liquor manufacturers are intentionally pitching their ads to teens is not important. The fact is, teenagers are watching and absorbing the message that drinking is a fun, cool, and popular thing to do. "You don't have to be a rocket scientist to understand that the intended—or unintended—consequences of these youthful liquor ads is that young people are going to drink more," says Dr. Edward Jacobs, a Seattle pediatrician and a member of the American Academy of Pediatrics' Committee on Substance Abuse. A company might say that they're just trying to get viewers to remember the product's name. But if that's the case, it seems unnecessary to spend millions per ad on directors, animation, and actors. "Why not simply put the name on a billboard?" asks Jacobs.

## What's the Big Deal?

So why is it such a problem if a teen starts drinking before age 21? Besides the fact that it's against the law, studies show that teens who begin drinking are four times as likely to become alcoholics as those who don't begin drinking before age 21. Alcohol is the drug most used and abused by adolescents— more than marijuana, heroin, cocaine, and pills combined. Students with grades below C are three times as likely to be drinkers as those with A's. Alcohol is usually a factor in the three leading causes of death among youth: accidents, suicide and homicide. Needless to say, drinking encourages reckless behavior.

"The major problem of drinking is not addiction," sums up Dr. Jacobs. "It's the consequence of use—the auto crashes, the lousy grades, the family problems and the sexual risk behaviors. Many times, these are the statistics that don't show up anywhere."

"I wouldn't say that kids would never drink if there were no ads," says 14-year-old Justin, a freshman at a suburban high school in Connecticut. "But the ads sure give kids a sense that drinking is just something you do—that it's part of normal life. What's mainstreamed is what we see on TV."

Dr. Jacobs agrees. "The ads send a uniform message: You can't get maximum pleasure from an activity without alcohol." It's easy to understand why a somewhat awkward teen who's trying to fit in would believe that alcohol will make him feel less clumsy.

To their credit, the major television stations have voluntarily banned ads for hard liquor (rum, vodka, scotch, etc.) for years. Earlier this year [2002] NBC announced that it would end its ban and allow ads for hard liquor. Months of criticism from legislators, the public, and advocacy groups forced the station to change that decision. Some say that TV stations should ban ads for beer and wine coolers, or at least monitor them to be sure they're not so youth-oriented. It's not as far-fetched as it seems. Sweden and Norway prohibit all advertising to children under 12. In Greece, commercials for toys can run only at certain hours, and Belgium forbids the running of commercials during children's programs and for five minutes before and after. Lawmakers in these countries understand that the very young are not yet mature enough to make critical choices when it comes to what they see advertised.

"Ads make it seem as if drinking is a very casual thing," says Justin. "Obviously, beer ads show people enjoying themselves. They don't show the negative consequences, like drunk driving or date rape. But sometimes, you know, it seems as if half my high school is in rehab."

## You Be the Judge

"Most of the ads for wine coolers and alcopops don't state or even imply that they have alcohol in them," says Dr. Jacobs. He's right. Media messages are created by people whose job it is to come up with interesting images, songs, or graphics that will make you want to buy their product. They do that by creating an image of the product or of the people who use it—often not telling the whole truth.

The next time you see an ad on TV, on the Web, or in print, take a moment to think about it.

Then answer the following questions:

- Is this ad telling the whole story? If not, what important information about the product is left out?—

- What image do the producers of this ad want me to have of this product?—

- If I use the product, will it make me look and act like the people in the ad?—

- If I were to write my own ad, what would I do differently?—

## The Alcohol Risk Factor

Teens who use and abuse alcohol are more likely to engage in other risky behavior that can be fatal. Check out these findings:

*Drinking and Driving*

Auto crashes are the No. 1 killer of teens. In one survey, 20 percent of the nearly 8,000 drivers ages 15 to 20 who were killed in auto crashes had been drinking.

*Suicide*

A correlation exists between alcohol use among teens and planning, attempting, or completing suicide. In one recent study, 37 percent of eighth grade girls who drank heavily reported attempting suicide.

*Sexual Behavior*

Twenty-nine percent of sexually active teens ages 15 to 17 reported in a survey that alcohol influenced their decision to have sex. And 26 percent of teens ages 15 to 17 said they worried about STDs or pregnancy because of becoming sexually active while drinking or using drugs.

*Violence*

Teens who drink are much more likely to engage in violence against others. One national survey found that of the teens who reported drinking regularly, 50 percent had been in a physical fight in the past year and 16 percent had carried a weapon to school in the past month. Other studies have found that alcohol plays a key role in violent crimes committed by teens, including murder, assault, and rape.

# 8

# Binge Drinking Is a Destructive Impulse

*Koren Zailckas*

*Koren Zailckas is the author of* Smashed: Story of a Drunken Girlhood.

*Early in her teens, Koren Zailckas relied on alcohol to overcome shyness. One night when she was 16, she drank so much at a friend's house that she had to be treated for alcohol blood poisoning. Although she told herself that she would drink more responsibly in the future, she continued to drink to excess for six more years. After a binge in Cancun, Mexico, Zailckas realized that she had to quit. Later she realized that because of alcohol abuse, she had missed the pleasures and pains of being a teenager.*

It was a cold Friday night in November, and I could see my breath between swigs of rum. It was a generic brand, and it had a strong acidic taste that bit my throat. I winced, coughed twice, and passed the jug to the girl beside me, who handed me back a bottle of Kahlua. I took a few candied gulps.

At 16, I was one of the dozens of kids in our Bolton, Massachusetts, suburb who came to Libby's backyard to party when her parents were away for the weekend. Maybe it's the same way in your town, kids drinking to get drunk every weekend—it's a social thing. Because Libby was afraid we'd spill alcohol on her mother's Venetian rugs, she wouldn't let anyone inside her house to mix drinks. Instead, we crowded on the splintered dock that hung over the lake in her back-yard and drank liquor straight from the bottle.

## The First Time

I'd actually had my first drink a couple of years earlier, when I was only 14. That time was at a friend's house too—she pulled out a whiskey bottle from a kitchen cabinet after school. Feeling the crisp liquid burn in my stomach made me feel like I was discovering a secret potion. Though I never liked the antiseptic taste of alcohol, I always loved drinking. Sober, I was a shy girl. But after two sips of hard liquor, I could usually speak without rehearsing the words in my head first. After four sips, I'd relax enough to lean my head against the person next to me. After six sips, I was brave enough to sing, do handstands, or pull off my bra through the sleeve of my coat when it pinched. The nausea that sometimes followed the next day was never fun, but it seemed a small price to pay for a personality boost.

## Near-Death Experience

For some reason, that particular night at Libby's, I just couldn't stir up a buzz. So I gulped more rum and chased it with more Kahlua. But that hot flush of confidence never came. My friend Claire passed me a thermos of straight vodka that had come from a bottle in her parents' liquor cabinet. It was the same bottle that we always stole from and then added water to to disguise our crime. After all the adding and subtracting, the vodka was tasteless. The last thing I remember is drinking it fast.

I'm told that minutes later, I tottered sideways and passed out on the dock. Claire said she jabbed me in the ribs and shouted in my ears, but nothing could wake me. She and three other girls carried me to the road by my arms and legs. They dropped me a few times. They draped me across the backseat of a car and drove me to my friend Abby's house. Because I'd already missed my curfew, Abby called my dad and told him I'd fallen asleep. She nervously asked if I could sleep over, but he asked to talk to me. By then I was throwing up in her sheets. When Abby held the receiver to my ear, I slurred, "I'll be home in 15 minutes, Daddy." He knew something was very wrong.

---

*It seemed cooler not to stop—everyone around me drank.*

---

When my dad got to Abby's, he put me in the car and rushed me to the hospital. Claire, who was an emergency medical trainee, came along to monitor my heart rate. She was terrified. When we reached the emergency room, my dad carried me through the sliding glass doors in his arms. The doctors said I was suffering from alcohol poisoning, caused by drinking a lot of alcohol in a short amount of time. My blood alcohol concentration, or the weight of alcohol present in 100 milliliters of my blood, was .25. A B.A.C. of .4 can kill an adult. The doctor said I would have died right there on the dock if I'd had a few more drinks. Later, Claire described to me the way the doctors passed a rubber tube through my nose, down my throat, and into my belly to pump my stomach. They funneled water through it, which made me vomit and emptied my stomach. The next morning, I woke up in my bedroom at home, still wearing a hospital gown. Purple bruises from being dragged and lifted flowered on my arms. My hair was in a pile of knots and sticky with vomit. I was paralyzed with fear. I lay in bed trying to figure out what had happened.

## The Morning After

At breakfast, my mother cried and my father looked at me with disbelief. My mom asked, "What if you fell into the water and drowned? What if you had been raped?" There wasn't much that I could say in my defense. Only "I'm so sorry."

After my experience with alcohol poisoning, I promised myself I'd "drink responsibly"—meaning I would still drink, but not to the point of oblivion. Yeah, right. For six more years I drank, and on too many nights to count I drank until I couldn't resist telling secrets to strangers or passing out wherever I happened to be. Does this sound familiar to you? I knew I should stop, but I didn't want to. It seemed cooler not to stop—everyone around me drank. I thought, Doesn't everyone everywhere? I wish I knew then how much that shouldn't have mattered. One spring break, I got so drunk in Cancun, Mexico, I lost my wallet, all my credit cards, and every dime I had. At 22, I woke up in a strange man's apartment after a binge. I realized that if the guy had been a killer—and if I had needed to call 911, I couldn't have even told them where I was. After that, I gave up drinking, cold.

## Facing the Real Me

After I quit drinking, it occurred to me that I'd never really grown up. It was a tough lesson to come by, because at 23 I'd never learned to deal with my shyness. I'd always used alcohol to mask it. I couldn't make eye contact with people or speak in public without my heart fluttering. The real tragedy about high school and college binge drinking is that we're robbed of all those authentic, vulnerable, growing-up moments. We lose years that we can never get back. So for me, sobriety has been about growing pains—finally living through my awkward phase. And being sober now allows me to share my story so that girls like me, maybe girls like you, might decide not to drink away their teens. These days I know the real Koren, and I'm beginning to think she's cool—without the buzz.

# 9

# Binge Drinking Is a Normal Impulse

*Jennie Bristow*

*Jennie Bristow is a commissioning editor for* Spiked Online *and has also written for* Living Marxism *and* Novo.

*When Britain liberalized alcohol laws at the beginning of 2005, public officials worried that binge drinking would become more prevalent. The fear seemed unreasonable: despite governmental warnings about alcohol abuse, British citizens were living longer and healthier lives than ever. The warnings, then, are less representative of a real threat than of a contemporary obsession with micro-managing society. A carefree drunk, emotional, talkative, and happy-go-lucky, conflicts with these idealized values. An occasional binge, however, is a good way for people to lose their inhibitions and escape—for a short time—from their everyday lives.*

What will British society look like under New Labour's proposed regime of licensing 24-hour drinking? Will it be the civilised café society of the political elite's dreams, where people sit around leisurely sipping from glasses of Chablis after a night at the theatre, or the anti-social dystopia of its nightmares, where teenagers spend all night out on the lash and schooldays snoozing at their desks?

Given the annual fad for debating the new licensing laws while doing nothing to change them, we may well never know. (Though a grasp of real life should tell us that the upshot will be neither dream nor nightmare, but really quite banal.) But the ongoing debate about the pros and cons of freeing pubs from their current 11pm shutdown is a sobering reflection on the kind of society we live in today—one that is too passion-less, uptight and risk-averse even to appreciate the importance of getting drunk.

Since the new year began, all 13 days ago [January 2005], we've been treated to headlined comments by medics, judges, politicians and policeman about the impact of the new licens-ing laws on individual health and public order. 'Binge drinking' (defined as more than two pints, and that's for the men) and 'anti-social behaviour' (defined as pretty much any-thing the authorities don't like) have become buzzwords in the phoney debate about whether it's better to have 11pm cur-fews or bars with no happy hours that stay open all hours but encourage their clients to take a pledge of sobriety. While the upper echelons of state and society wrangle over the best way of regulating drinking, agreement is taken for granted on the key goal: Drunkenness Reduction. To which somebody, surely, has to ask—why?

What is it about getting drunk that today's society finds so hard to handle? It isn't as though we live in a nation of feck-less alcoholics, too sodden to pour themselves out of bed and into work in the morning. For all the government's dire warn-ings about rising rates of liver cirrhosis and general alcohol-related health calamities, we should remember (again) that in reality, we are living longer and healthier lives than ever be-fore.

And Britain 2005 is hardly a hotbed of inebriated violence. On 11 January [2005], a judge grabbed the headlines by at-tacking legalised 24-hour drinking on the grounds that easy access to alcohol is breeding 'urban savages' and turning town centres into no-go areas. The basis for his claim? That he was sentencing three men convicted of vicious assaults while out drinking and drug-taking after the European Championships, which left one of their victims in a coma. Maybe this judge knows more about town centres and urban savagery than the rest of us—even so, he surely must believe that behaviour like that above is the exception rather than the rule.

## Losing Our Inhibitions

What we do have is a society in which sometimes, and for a variety of reasons, people like to drink to get drunk. Not because they think that wine goes better with dinner than Ribena [a British fruit drink]; not because they want to relax a little after a hard day's white-collar work; not because they believe the studies about a glass of red being good for their hearts (but two pints of lager being very bad indeed); but because they want to get off the plane of existence that is normal, humdrum, everyday life, and into that parallel universe of inebriation. What's wrong with doing that once in a while? Nothing. Indeed, there is a good deal that is very right about it.

*We know that, every now and then, one very important reason to drink is to get drunk.*

The key feature of alcohol, and the one that most worries today's uptight political class, is that it makes people lose their inhibitions. They become more aggressive, or more vulnerable to date-raping predators; they stop caring about what is good for their health or personal finances; they talk to strangers and pick arguments with their friends. In one night down the pub, these people, docilely on-message by day, manage to cock a snook at every principle of our carefully managed Therapeutic Society. Emotions rage, passions roar, and if it all ends in tears they are the messy, uncontrolled ones of the drunkard rather than the controlled closures of the counselling room. And for what? So they can wake up with a pounding hangover and a shiver of embarrassment, having achieved nothing more worthy than a good night out.

It is not the consequences of drunkenness that make it a modern bogeyman, but its simple out-of-controlness. For a political class hell-bent on micro-management of all aspects of everyday life, in thrall to etiquette, suspicious of spontaneity, and living by the code of 'everything in moderation', the image of the carefree drunk is one that it cannot comprehend, still less empathise with. For the rest of us, for whom the odd bender is not a political statement but a welcome fact of life, we should resist the temptation to buy into the cult of 'responsible drinking' and remember what we are doing in the pub in the first place.

Already, there are too many twentysomething women on broken detox diets crying into their alcopops about how they know they drink too much. There are too many single men staying 'just for the one' before driving home to their X-box and pizza-and-Pepsi meal deal. There is too much consensus that we need to change the licensing laws because we have a cultural 'drinking problem' (rather than simply changing the law to allow us to have a drink when we want it). There is too much no smoking at the bar, no swearing at the bar, no standing at the bar and no going to the bar too many times.

We know that, every now and then, one very important reason to drink is to get drunk. We know that people with lost inhibitions generally don't get raped, beaten up or bankrupt, but generally do become sexier, funnier, more honest and more sociable (even if they appeal only to other drunk people). And we know that humdrum everyday life is often better escaped from in a pub with colleagues, friends and strangers than obsessed upon over a nice bottle of wine with a therapist or mentor.

So let's leave the official preoccupations with when we drink, how much we drink and why we drink to the medics, judges, politicians and policemen, and carry on drinking as we choose.

# 10

# Parents Are Accountable for Children's Alcohol Abuse

*Shari Roan*

*Shari Roan is a staff writer for the* Los Angeles Times.

*It has become common to prosecute parents for allowing teens access to alcohol. While many believe that teens gain access to alcohol by using fake IDs, the Monitoring the Future survey reveals that more teens obtain alcohol from their homes. Although parents may believe that it is better to regulate alcohol in the home, they are probably unaware of the dangers alcohol abuse poses to teens. Underage drinking can lead to violence, poor school performance, and brain damage. Parents and teens need to be educated on the dangers of alcohol abuse.*

Teenagers who have consumed alcohol die every week in the United States, most often in car crashes. But when a 16-year-old boy died in Asheville, N.C., in April, Buncombe County Dist. Atty. Ron Moore decided he'd seen enough.

After investigating the incident, he charged 17 people for alcohol violations committed at a party the teenager had attended before driving drunk. Among those charged were adults who had hosted the party and another adult who had allegedly purchased beer for the teens.

"I hope it will deter adults from providing the alcohol and making it easy for kids to get," says Moore of the charges. "Hopefully, word will get around that if you're an adult and you serve alcohol and something happens, you'll be held accountable."

Across the nation, legislatures and law enforcement agencies have been increasingly willing to hold adults responsible for underage drinking and the problems such drinking creates. Now a new survey of teens and parents underscores the difficulties they face.

In the study, released today [August 8, 2005], underage drinkers said they found it easy to obtain alcohol from an adult, particularly at parties. More than one-fourth of the teens said they had attended a party where kids consumed alcohol with parents present. And almost one-third of the teens said it was easy to get alcohol from their parents with their parents' knowledge.

---

*About one-forth of the parents polled in the study said they have allowed their teens to drink alcohol in the last six months.*

---

Far fewer teens reported getting alcohol using riskier methods, such as trying to buy it themselves or using a fake ID. Teen girls were found to be more effective than teen boys at obtaining alcohol, possibly because girls often date or socialize with older males who have access to alcohol.

The results confirm how easy it is for teens to obtain alcohol from adults, either with their permission or surreptitiously. The Monitoring the Future survey conducted by the University of Michigan has found that, nationwide, about 75% of high school seniors and 39% of eighth-graders say they have consumed alcohol in the last year.

## Where Teens Get Alcohol

"The perception out there is that 90% of teens get alcohol using fake IDs and by going to bars. That's not true," says Dr. J. Edward Hill, president of the American Medical [Association]. "They are getting it from social sources: parents, older friends, older siblings and others. Parents need to become aware of the fact that a large percentage of alcohol comes from their own homes or the homes of other parents."

---

*Research shows underage drinking plays a large part in teen crime, violence, sexual activity and accidents.*

---

The survey, from the American Medical Assn., involved 701 teens ages 13 to 18 and 2,283 adults, of whom 394 were parents of children ages 12 to 20.

Many of the adults displayed a nonchalant attitude about teen drinking. About one-fourth of the parents polled in the study said they have allowed their teens to drink alcohol in the last six months.

"The rationalization among parents is teens are going to do it anyway, let them do it under my supervision," says Pat Hines, executive director of Safe Moves, a Los Angeles non-profit program on traffic safety education that recently developed a program for teens on drinking and driving. "Parents think they can control it. I think that's a fallacy. [Drinking] becomes almost acceptable when a parent establishes those parameters."

Parents may not understand the toll of underage drinking, Hill says. Research shows underage drinking plays a large part in teen crime, violence, sexual activity and accidents. Underage drinking can lead to addiction or other substance abuse, affect school performance and even damage the developing brain.

"A child who begins to drink before the legal drinking age may end up having a significant problem with reasoning and memory because of their alcohol use," says Hill. "That kid is not going to do as well in school. Parents are not as aware [of the consequences] as they should be."

The alcohol industry should be included in efforts to hold adults more responsible, Hill says.

"The industry says, 'Talk to your kids about drinking.' But they are out there advertising to kids. They are the ones that make parents' jobs so difficult," he says.

Education needs to be aimed at adults and teens to curb the use of alcohol, Hines says. Hines' new program, called Wheel Smarts, uses plays and staged "crime scene investigations" to prompt teens to think about the consequences of alcohol use. It is funded by the California Office of Traffic Safety and is offered to Los Angeles-area middle and high schools.

"Parents can lay down the law, but kids are still going to do what they want," she says. "The solution truly is education aimed at the parents and the kids, because the kids are the ones who are going to get behind the wheel. But education is expensive, and it's hard work."

In Buncombe County, the adults charged in the incident are awaiting trial, Moore says. He says he may allow some of the youths charged with underage drinking to perform some type of community service. "To me, one of the ways to try to address this problem is more education of teenagers."

*Where Teens Get Alcohol*

Teenagers have little difficulty obtaining alcohol, finds a survey sponsored by the American Medical Assn., with adults often complicit in the process.

Percentage of teenagers saying it was easy to get alcohol through the following sources:

*At a party*: 80%

*From their home (without their parents' knowledge)*: 67%

*From relatives or a brother/sister who is older than 21*: 65%

*From someone else's parent(s)*: 40%

*Using a fake ID*: 36%

*From their parents (with their parents' knowledge)*: 32%

# 11

# Parents Should Be Allowed to Regulate Children's Use of Alcohol

*Marsha Rosenbaum*

*Marsha Rosenbaum is the author of* Safety First: A Reality-Based Approach to Teens, Drugs, and Drug Education. *She is a director for the Drug Policy Alliance in San Francisco.*

*It has become common in the United States to prosecute parents for allowing teens access to alcohol. Unfortunately, these policies may create new problems. While many parents may prefer their teens to abstain from alcohol use, they have reluctantly decided that it is safer for their teens to drink at home. At parties and other functions away from home, teens often choose to drive while under the influence of alcohol. By punishing parents, it is more likely that teens, away from home, will become involved in unsafe behavior like driving drunk.*

In the aftermath of a New Year's Eve party involving underage drinking, a dentist and his wife from the affluent New York suburb of Scarsdale have been charged with "first degree unlawfully dealing with a child," a misdemeanor, and are being arraigned Feb. 8 [2005].

The couple may serve a year in jail for allowing teenagers to imbibe in their home. This is not an isolated incident. In communities all over the country, from California to Florida to Illinois to Vermont, state and local "social host" laws such

Marsha Rosenbaum, "Prosecuting Mom and Dad," *AlterNet*, January 19, 2005. Reproduced by permission.

as the one used to charge the Scarsdale couple are furtively being passed in an effort to put a stop to teenage alcohol use, making criminals out of otherwise responsible, law-abiding parents all across America.

As an alcohol and drug abuse expert and the mother of four, I worry that out of frustration, fear, and desperation, criminal justice efforts to eliminate underage drinking, targeted at parents, may actually worsen the situation and reduce teen safety.

It is imperative to first look at the context of drinking in America. Alcohol has always been America's drug of choice—the substance we use to celebrate (*Let's drink to that!*), recreate (*I can't wait to kick back and have a cold one*), and medicate (*Man, I really need a drink*).

Although we may not approve, it's worth remembering that teenage alcohol use is nothing new. It's been a part of American culture since the first Puritan settlers in the 17th century, and has worried parents since that time. As City University of New York professor Harry G. Levine, an eminent alcohol historian, told me, "For 400 years, adult Americans have drunk alcoholic drinks—rum, ale, corn whiskey, lager beer, roaring '20s cocktails, gin, wine, scotch, vodka, and nowadays piña coladas in cans. And for 400 years, each generation of American parents have [sic] also worried about the drinking and drunkenness of their teenaged children and fretted about their incapacity to eliminate it, or even reduce it. None of that is new. But the riskiness of teenage drinking is greater now than in the past because of our reliance on automobiles."

## Safer at Home

Indeed, the most lethal aspect of underage alcohol use, by far, is drunk driving, with the National Highway Safety Administration reporting in 2003 that nearly 2,400 teens died in car accidents involving alcohol and far more were seriously injured. It is for this very reason that some parents, particularly in suburban communities where so many young people drive, have reluctantly permitted their teens to drink at home.

---

*Sending parents to jail for trying to keep their teenagers safe is not the answer, and it may ultimately do more harm than good.*

---

Alcohol use by a sizable number of teenagers is not likely to go away any time soon. In fact, last month's annual survey, Monitoring the Future, revealed that once again alcohol overwhelmingly topped the list of teenagers' drugs of choice, with 77 percent trying it at some point during their high school years and 60 percent having gotten drunk—30 percent within the past month.

In my work as a drug researcher and educator, I have spoken confidentially with hundreds of parents who have strongly encouraged their teens to abstain, assessed the reality of this request, and then reluctantly provided their home as a safe space to gather. . . . These parents do not condone or promote drinking. Nor do they provide or serve alcohol at parties. But they understand that underage drinking will occur, whether or not they approve. The difficult decision they make has driving in the forefront of their minds. They confiscate car keys and keep an eye out for problems, believing their teens are safer at home where they can be supervised, than on the road.

I hate to see safety-oriented parents vilified, but worry even more about the teenagers they're trying to protect. When I ask young people how they'll respond to the proliferation of these local ordinances, which will effectively eliminate the availability of parentally supervised homes where they can "hang out," not one says they'll stop drinking. Instead, they say they will simply move the party to the street, the local park, the beach or some other public place. And they'll get there by car.

Before there are more car accidents and other alcohol-related problems, we should reassess our approach to under-age drinking. Obviously, abstinence would be the safest choice. In the meantime, comprehensive alcohol education is imperative, as are crackdowns on drunk driving. But let's get real. There will always be parties, and while we encourage and promote sober gatherings, parents should have a fallback strategy that makes sure drinking and driving don't mix. Sending parents to jail for trying to keep their teenagers safe is not the answer, and it may ultimately do more harm than good.

# 12

# Eliminating Drunk Driving Is a Reasonable Goal

*Mothers Against Drunk Driving*

*Mothers Against Drunk Driving (MADD) works to prevent drunk driving and prevent underage drinking.*

*Mothers Against Drunk Driving (MADD) announced a campaign to totally eliminate drunk driving in 2006. By utilizing technology, new laws, grass roots mobilization, and vigorous enforcement, MADD envisioned a new assault on drunk driving, which continues to cost 13,000 lives per year. MADD, along with a number of private and governmental organizations, promised to work toward these goals. In addition to these efforts, research focused on new technology may also offer new ways to eliminate drunk driving. While no single method will eliminate drunk driving, a combination of methods, along with multiple organizations working toward the same goal, offers the most promising strategy.*

In a bold new effort designed to eradicate one of the nation's deadliest crimes, Mothers Against Drunk Driving (MADD) today launched its national *Campaign to Eliminate Drunk Driving*, which aims to literally wipe out drunk driving in the United States.

Despite a more than 40 percent decline in alcohol-related traffic fatalities since MADD was founded in 1980, the threat still remains. Every year, nearly 13,000 people are killed by drunk drivers with an illegal blood alcohol concentration

Mothers Against Drunk Driving, "MADD Announces National Campaign to Eliminate Drunk Driving," www.madd.org, November 20, 2006. Reproduced by permission.

(BAC) of .08 or above, and countless others are injured. This represents more than 1,000 families every month that must live with the tragic consequences of drunk driving.

"The real possibility of eliminating drunk driving in this country is a powerful, even audacious, idea. Yet the tools are now at hand. Using technology, tougher enforcement, stronger laws and grassroots mobilization, the goal of eliminating a primary public health threat that has plagued the United States is within our reach," said Glynn Birch, national president of MADD, whose 21-month-old son was killed by a drunk driver in 1988.

As a nation, our efforts to prevent drunk-driving fatalities have stalled. MADD's plan to eliminate this public health threat requires new strategies to complement current methods. Today, MADD is announcing a 4-point plan to lead the nation toward the goals of eliminating drunk driving:

- *Intensive high-visibility law enforcement,* including twice-yearly crackdowns and frequent enforcement efforts that include sobriety checkpoints and saturation patrols in all 50 states;

- *Full implementation of current alcohol ignition interlock technologies,* including efforts to require alcohol ignition interlock devices for all convicted drunk drivers. A key part of this effort will be working with judges, prosecutors and state driver's license officials to stop the revolving door of repeat offenders;

- *Exploration of advanced vehicle technologies through the establishment of a Blue Ribbon panel of international safety experts to assess the feasibility of a range of technologies that would prevent drunk driving.* These technologies must be moderately priced, absolutely reliable, set at the legal BAC limit and unobtrusive to the sober driver; and

- *Mobilization of grassroots support,* led by MADD and its 400+ affiliates, to make the elimination of drunk driving a reality. MADD is uniting drunk driving victims, families, community leaders, and policy makers in the fight to eliminate drunk driving.

With emerging technology, the vision that drunk drivers will not be able to operate vehicles is no longer a dream but, with substantial research, a real possibility. But to achieve it, all four strategies must succeed. Interlock use must expand to all convicted drunk drivers. Emerging technologies must be developed into effective and practical devices that don't inhibit lawful drivers. High-visibility enforcement must continue. All three of these components must be backed up by effective communications and broad public support.

## A United Effort Against Drunk Driving

U.S. Secretary of Transportation Mary E. Peters said, "Drunk driving is a problem that is painful and persistent, but it's also preventable. Pairing the public and private sectors for the common good is a powerful combination, one that will help us achieve real results in terms of saving lives and preventing injuries."

Secretary Peters was joined at the event by NHTSA Administrator Nicole Nason, who is the Honorary Chair of the *Campaign to Eliminate Drunk Driving.*

Joining MADD at the press conference were the Department of Transportation, the National Highway Traffic Safety Administration (NHTSA), the Insurance Institute for Highway Safety (IIHS), the Governors Highway Safety Association (GHSA), the Century Council, the Distilled Spirits Council of the United States (DISCUS), the International Association of Chiefs of Police (IACP), and the Alliance of Automobile Manufacturers. Properly implemented, this public/private partnership will lead to the elimination of one of the primary public health threats to the American family for the last 100 years. Each supporter will pursue these initiatives according to their own policies and procedures.

Lt. Colonel Jim Champagne, immediate past chairman of GHSA, endorsed the *Campaign* as a way to renew attention to the drunk driving problem. According to Champagne, "State Highway Safety Agencies were pleased to work with MADD to help develop this new *Campaign* and we think it sends a clear message to those who may be tempted to drive drunk: we will use every tool at our disposal to keep our roads safe and when we arrest you—and we will—there will be no leniency."

Highly visible law enforcement crackdowns, including checkpoints and saturation patrols, are proven to get drunk drivers off the road. Eighty-seven percent of Americans support the use of sobriety checkpoints, yet 10 states still prohibit the use of them. The *Campaign* will work to make checkpoints legal in all states.

"Impaired driving is not just another traffic offense; it is a serious crime that often causes needless deaths and injuries," said IACP President Joseph Carter, Chief of the MBTA Transit Police Department. "More than two decades of research have demonstrated that sobriety checkpoints and other law enforcement efforts make a difference. They are vitally effective techniques to get impaired drivers off of our roads."

Research shows that the overwhelming majority of people arrested for drunk driving have driven drunk more than 50 times *before their first arrest*. Two-thirds of those whose licenses are suspended for DUI [driving under the influence] drive anyway. Interlocks are proven to be up to 90 percent effective while on the vehicle, yet it is estimated that only one in eight convicted drunk drivers each year currently get the device, and most of those are repeat offenders. Sixty-five percent of the public support mandatory interlocks for first time offenders, and 85 percent of the public support mandatory interlocks for repeat offenders.

The Honorable Susan Molinari, chairman of The Century Council, noted, "I thank MADD for having the vision that eliminating drunk driving is possible and that to do it, it requires many different stakeholders at the table. By working together, we can eliminate drunk driving."

## New Technology

In addition to stronger enforcement and mandatory interlocks for all convicted drunk drivers, MADD supports the development of new sensor technology already underway that allows a vehicle to recognize if a driver is drunk, and to stop the driver from operating that vehicle. The public is overwhelmingly supportive: by a 4 to 1 margin (58 percent to 16 percent), Americans support advances in smart vehicle technology to prevent drunk driving.

"Enforcement is essential, but we know we'll never arrest all drunk drivers once they get on the road," said Susan Ferguson, senior vice president of research at the Insurance Institute for Highway Safety and chair of the newly-announced Blue Ribbon Panel for the Development of Advanced Alcohol Detection Technology. "If society is to eliminate the carnage caused by drunk drivers, we must do more to prevent them from drinking and driving in the first place. Fortunately, advanced technology is being developed that may allow quick, reliable detection to do just that."

---

*There is no single solution that will eliminate drunk driving.*

---

MADD, NHTSA, the auto industry and the Insurance Institute for Highway Safety are forming a cooperative research initiative via the Blue Ribbon Panel for the Development of Advanced Alcohol Detection Technology to help bring this new technology to market in the next 10 years through a non-regulator, voluntary and data driven effort.

"The Institute has long studied the most effective ways to enforce alcohol-impaired driving laws," adds Adrian Lund, president of IIHS. "Now our research will have two broad objectives: to maximize the effectiveness of laws and enforcement techniques and to study how new technology can fit seamlessly into the driving task without affecting the majority of drivers who drive sober."

At least four classes of technology warrant further investigation by the Blue Ribbon Panel: advanced breath testing, both individual testing and testing for alcohol in the vehicle; using visible light to measure BAC (spectroscopy); using non-invasive touch-based systems to measure BAC transdermally; and eye movement measurement technology, including the involuntary eye movements (or nystagmus) related to BAC, and eye closure that can indicate drowsiness.

"There is no single solution that will eliminate drunk driving. Drunk driving remains a behavioral challenge, an enforcement challenge and a challenge requiring innovative new approaches, including exploring new technologies," said Fred Webber, president & CEO, Alliance of Automobile Manufacturers. "These diverse organizations are well suited to address the long-term strategy."

MADD intends to work with law enforcement agencies, judicial organizations, auto manufacturers, insurers, distilled spirits companies, technology companies, safety advocates, health care professionals, and emergency technicians to abolish drunk driving in the U.S. through the *Campaign to Eliminate Drunk Driving*.

# 13

# Eliminating Drunk Driving Creates Repressive Laws

*Radley Balko*

*Radley Balko is a columnist for Fox News and a former analyst for the Cato Institute.*

*Because of the efforts of Mothers Against Drunk Driving (MADD) in the early 1980s, attitudes have changed toward driving under the influence. As a result, traffic fatalities have decreased; however, after reaching these goals, MADD has continued to push for more reforms, reforms that sometimes eliminate important legal protections. With misleading statistics, advocates like MADD have increasingly shifted their concern from drunk driving to drinking and driving. Lowering the alcohol blood level to .08 percent is representative of the shift. Statistics show that these social drinkers are seldom the cause of accidents; furthermore, the stricter laws increase enforcement costs with no discernible benefit. Sobriety checkpoints, for example, crack down on social drinkers and absorb law enforcement's time with little evident effect. Legal rulings involving checkpoints have also reduced constitutional protections. This series of actions reveals that many organizations are no longer campaigning against drunk driving but against drinking itself.*

Perhaps the boldest front on which the neoprohibition effort has been moving is drunk driving—or, more accurately now, *drinking* and driving. Since the early 1980s, organi-

Radley Balko, "Back Door to Prohibition: The New War on Social Drinking," *Policy Analysis*, December 5, 2003, pp. 9–16. Copyright © 2003 Cato Institute. All rights reserved. Reproduced by permission.

zations such as Mothers Against Drunk Driving have waged aggressive, high-profile, ubiquitous campaigns to raise public awareness of a formidable threat to public safety that far too few people take seriously.

The campaign was enormously successful. Alcohol-related traffic deaths have dropped by 40 percent since 1982, even as non-alcohol-related traffic fatalities have increased by 39 percent. The total number of victims of drunk drivers has stabilized since the mid-1990s. The percentage of drivers who had blood alcohol levels above the legal limit dropped from 27 percent in 1991 to 21 percent in 2001. Among underage drivers—often cited by temperance advocates as a reason to restrict access to alcohol—there was a similar decrease. The number of drivers involved in fatal accidents who were intoxicated dropped by 24 percent between 1991 and 2001.

In short, attitudes have changed. Today's drunk driver is a pariah. It is no longer socially acceptable to stagger out from a pub and slip behind the wheel. Chuck Hurley, a spokesman for the National Safety Council—which advocates tougher drinking and driving laws—has said: "We've already deterred virtually all of the social drinkers. We're now down to the hard core of people who drink and drive in spite of public scorn." Former MADD president Katherine Prescott agreed, telling the *New York Times* that the problem "has been reduced to a hard core of alcoholics who do not respond to public appeal." Unfortunately, those conclusions seem to run counter to the policies being pushed by Hurley and Prescott's organizations, as well as the other key players in the temperance movement. And, increasingly, those policies are finding warm receptions in state legislatures.

## Criminalizing Drinkers

In 2002 and 2003 alone, more than 100 new pieces of legislation further restricting already stringent drinking and driving parameters were introduced in 31 different states. Some of those laws were reasonable, of course—increasing fines for repeat offenders, for example. But others attempted to strip drunk-driving suspects of legitimate criminal protections. One law introduced in Virginia attempted to do away with the practice of making a blood sample available to the defendant for independent testing after a first sample used by law enforcement revealed an illegal level of intoxication. Laws like these find support from the public because temperance advocates and their supporters in government have been enormously successful in propagating the idea that drunk driving still poses an increasing threat to public safety, despite the figures cited above.

One example of how those advocating tougher drinking and driving laws have manipulated data is the touting of a figure they call "alcohol-related fatalities." The National Traffic Highway Safety Administration uses this number each year in its Fatality Analysis Reporting System. The problem with the term "alcohol-related," however, is that it's based on statistical modeling and creates an impression among the public that's at odds with what it actually represents. Most hear "alcohol-related fatalities" and assume "fatalities caused by drunk drivers." In truth, "alcohol-related" fatalities include any accident in which alcohol was even remotely involved.

"Alcohol-related" fatalities include accidents in which a drunk driver was killed by the negligence of a sober driver, a drunk passenger was killed in a car driven by or hit by a sober driver, a drunk pedestrian was killed by a sober driver, and even all of the previous scenarios when the actors weren't even legally drunk but had merely consumed any amount of alcohol at all. The number can even include accidents in which there's no evidence of alcohol but under circumstances in which alcohol is commonly involved, such as a lone driver crashing his car in the early hours of the morning.

In 2001 NHTSA [National Highway Traffic Safety Administration] claimed 17,448 people were killed in alcohol-related traffic accidents. A *Los Angeles Times* investigation conducted in December 2002 looked at that number, looked at a sampling of accident reports, and dismissed NHTSA's statistical modeling mechanism. Disallowing for the myriad scenarios in which it couldn't be conclusively proven that a drunk driver's negligence was to blame, the *Los Angeles Times* found that about 5,000 of those 17,448 traffic deaths in 2001 involved a sober person killed by a drunk driver. The investigation detailed one accident in Aliceville, Alabama, where a state trooper merely suspected that a driver had been drinking. Though no alcohol test was ever performed, and the family of the victim later contended in a lawsuit that the accident was the result of a rollover defect, the fatality was still attributed to alcohol by NHTSA.

Perhaps most revealing of the campaign against social drinking is the way the language of public officials and anti-alcohol advocates has changed. "Drunks" have been replaced by "drinkers," "drunk driving" by "drinking and driving." It's a subtle change, but a significant one. Attempting to demonize the mix of driving with *any* amount of alcohol consumption is a clear departure from a campaign focused on highway safety. It is an effort to more generally change the drinking behavior of Americans. No drinking and driving means no beer or two at the ball-game before coming home, no after-dinner Irish coffee, no glass of wine with a dinner out. Consider:

- A series of taxpayer-funded radio ads in Washington, DC, told motorists, "If you're still drinking and driving, the new [lower blood-alcohol threshold] law is aimed right at you. Never drink and drive."

- A joint campaign undertaken by MADD and the U.S. Department of Transportation was titled "You Drink & Drive. You Lose." U.S. Transportation Secretary Norm Mineta said during the campaign: "If you drink and drive, you lose. If we catch you drinking and driving, we will arrest you and prosecute you."

- At that same campaign kickoff, William B. Berger, former president of the International Association of Chiefs of Police, declared, "We will not allow a man or woman to leave [a sobriety checkpoint] knowing they consumed alcohol." Note Berger's choice of words—not that "they are drunk," merely that "they consumed alcohol."

- DOT [Department of Transportation] also released to local law enforcement officials a kit of information on how to initiate the details of the campaign. "The campaign's message is a simple one," the kit says, "don't drive after drinking alcohol. . . ."

- The American Beverage Institute conducted a survey of driver manuals at various state departments of motor vehicles. California, for example, scolds that "one drink can make you an unsafe driver." Kentucky and Massachusetts say that "one drink will affect your driving." Nevada warns, "There is no safe way to drive after drinking." Oregon cautions, "ANY level of alcohol in your blood impairs to some degree your ability to drive."

- The state of Virginia just approved $500,000 for a radio advertising campaign to air 22,000 total ads on 52 stations incorrectly telling listeners that "it's illegal to drink and drive."

## Lowering the Blood Alcohol Concentration Level

The most prominent law that exemplifies the shift from "drunk driving" to "drinking and driving" was signed by President Clinton in 2000. That federal law (frequently referred to as .08 per se) encouraged states to lower the legal blood alcohol concentration (BAC), measured in percentages, from .10 to .08. That means that, as of October 2003, drivers with a BAC of .08 or higher were automatically assumed to be intoxicated. Any state that does not make the policy change will lose federal highway funds.

Since that law went into effect, all but six states—Minnesota, Colorado, New Jersey, Delaware, Nevada, and West Virginia—have complied with the .08 mandate. A few states put up a fight. Iowa State Senate Majority Leader Steward Iverson called the federal .08 law "blackmail." "Why is .08 the magic number? By lowering it to .08, we are going to catch more of what I call the social drinkers. I had two friends killed by drunk drivers, but we have to be realistic." Ohio State Senate President Richard Fenan told the *Los Angeles Times*, "The people who have had a few beers or a glass of wine are not the problem. We call it prohibition drip by drip. It is prohibitionists who want this. Their goal is zero tolerance."

The most obvious objection to .08 per se is that it does little to improve highway safety. It will of course increase the number of "drunk" driving arrests because it increases the pool of "drunks" by redefining what it means to be drunk, but there's no significant evidence to suggest that removing drivers who register between .08 and .10 will save lives. In fact, the available evidence suggests otherwise:

- California was one of the first states to implement .08 per se, and a study conducted a year later by the state's Department of Motor Vehicles found that the law's "effect was primarily limited to individuals who generally restrict their alcohol consumption before driving anyway."

- California's alcohol-related fatality rates did drop the first year .08 per se was implemented, but at a rate (6.1 percent) that was lower than the national average (6.3 percent).

- Only 2 of the 10 states with the lowest traffic fatality rates in 2000 had at that time adopted .08 per se. Traffic fatality statistics offer further evidence of the futility of .08 per se:

- Two-thirds of the drivers in alcohol-related fatal accidents have a BAC of .14 or higher. The average BAC in fatal accidents involving alcohol is .17.

- In the last 15 years, more drivers registering BAC levels of .01 to .03 caused fatal accidents than did drivers with BACs from .08 to .10.

- A National Highway Traffic Safety Administration study of the first five states to adopt .08 per se measured the impact of the law in 30 different highway safety categories. States with .08 cumulatively got "safer" in 9 of the 30 categories but were unchanged or "less safe" in the remaining 21.

- Looking abroad, Sweden has a BAC threshold of .02, yet the average BAC in alcohol-related fatal accidents there is still .15.

To this day NHTSA claims that a nationwide .08 per se rule would save 500 lives per year, a number still cited by MADD and other anti-alcohol groups across the country. The Clinton administration cited that number when promoting the federal .08 law. Numerous state government agencies also cited that number in passing .08 laws before the 2003 deadline. But the 500 number is based on a study by longtime anti-alcohol activist Ralph Hingson, a former vice president of MADD. In 1999 the U.S. General Accounting Office [GAO] looked at Hingson's report and his "500 lives saved" conclusion and declared it "unfounded."

The GAO has looked at several studies NHTSA has done on the effectiveness of .08 per se and concluded that "the evidence does not conclusively establish that .08 BAC laws by themselves result in reductions in the number and severity of crashes involving alcohol . . . NHTSA's position—that the evidence was conclusive—was overstated." Yet NHTSA's position on .08 per se continues to be the official position of the federal government, and its studies are still touted by state legislators, activists, and editorial boards that support .08, despite the GAO's critical assessments.

The National Motorists Association reports another statistical fudge employed by MADD and NHTSA to promote .08 per se. Previously, BAC charts issued by both organizations showed .08 as the reasonable BAC a normal person could expect to hit after two or three drinks in an hour. NMA reports that a new series of charts issued by MADD and NHTSA after the federal .08 law passed changed the scale a bit. The new charts say a 180-pound person needs *five* drinks to hit .08. But the new charts stretch the allotted time for those five drinks from one hour to three. Nevertheless, when trying to convince a state legislator to lower BAC limits, it's more persuasive to say a that 180-pound person needs five drinks to hit .08 than two or three because it allays concerns about criminalizing moderate social drinking.

The preponderance of the evidence, then, suggests that lowering the legal BAC threshold from .10 to .08 does little to address the primary alcohol-related threat to highway safety— the hard drinkers who cause most of the accidents. It's akin to lowering the speed limit from 65 to 50 in order to catch people who regularly drive 100 mph. The new "criminals" really aren't the problem, and targeting them diverts valuable law enforcement resources from catching the people who are.

In Minnesota lawmakers decided that the amount of money it would cost the state to prosecute drivers who weren't a threat to public safety would exceed the amount of federal funding the state would forego by not adopting .08. State legislator Tom Rukavina told the *Los Angeles Times* that .08 per se would result in about 6,000 new criminal arrests at a cost of about $60 million to the state. That was more than Minnesota would give up from the federal government if it kept its .10 standard. Nevada legislators voted down .08 for similar reasons.

Yet $40 million of NHTSA's $225 million in highway traffic safety grants is specifically earmarked for "Alcohol-Impaired Driving Countermeasures Incentive Grants designed to encourage states to pass strong anti-drunk-driving legislation." An additional $41 million of its operations and research budget is designated for "impaired driving deterrence." That is in addition to whatever portions of other budgetary items find their way to drunk-driving deterrence programs. The *Los Angeles Times* estimates that the agency spends as much as $300 million—more than half its budget—on fighting drinking and driving. Critics look at those numbers and question why NHTSA devotes so much of its budget to a problem that's been on the decline for a quarter century, while sober-driver highway fatalities far outnumber alcohol-related fatalities and have increased by nearly 40 percent in the last 20 years.

The .08 per se laws grow more absurd when one compares the amount of impairment that may be attributable to a .08 BAC with that caused by other activities motorists routinely engage in while driving:

- In 1997 the *New England Journal of Medicine* published a study concluding that drivers using cellular phones experienced the same amount of impairment as those with a BAC of .10.

- A study by Britain's Transport Research Laboratory found that drivers using handheld phones had reaction times 30 percent slower than drivers impaired by a .08 BAC. And an American Automobile Association study conducted in 2001 found that cellular phone use was less of a distraction to drivers than, among other things, having children in the back seat, eating while driving, or fumbling with a CD or radio tuner.

Forty-five of the 50 states (plus the District of Columbia and Puerto Rico) have enacted laws requiring the suspension of driver's licenses and even jail time for motorists who are no more impaired than most of us are on our commute to and from work, simply because the impairment happens to be induced by drinking instead of something less socially stigmatized.

And there's little reason to think the effort will stop at .08. Different people absorb alcohol into the bloodstream at different rates, but by most estimates a 120-pound woman can easily get to .08 by drinking two glasses of wine in two hours. If .08 doesn't represent significant driver impairment, it's troubling to think that the threshold could fall even lower. But statements from public officials and anti-alcohol activists and some laws already enacted suggest movement in that direction:

- MADD Canada recently unveiled its campaign to initiate a .05 national standard. The organization conducted a poll showing that 66 percent of Canadians support the idea.

- Minnesota DWI [driving while intoxicated] Task Force chairman Steve Simon said in 1997 that "ultimately, it [the BAC threshold] should be .02 percent."

- The state of Michigan has set a BAC limit of .02 percent for any state officials on duty.

- In North Royalton, Ohio, police can cite motorists with a "physical control violation" for the mere smell of alcohol in a vehicle.

- Legislators in Arkansas and New Mexico have proposed .07 and .06 limits, respectively; and Delaware State Rep. William Oberle, when submitting his bill to move the state to .08, expressed his desire for "zero tolerance, like they have in Europe." An advocacy group also points out that at least six other states have considered legislation moving the BAC threshold below .08.

- An editorial in Utah's *Deseret News* called for the state—which was the first to enact .08—to lower its BAC threshold to .02, not because it would make highways safer, but because it would effect a "cultural shift" in attitudes about alcohol.

- Former Illinois state senator Robert Molaro says, "I think 40 years from now, our grandchildren and our great-grand-children are going to say, 'You mean we used to let people have a beer or two and go drive a car?'"

- California Sen. Barbara Boxer has said, "I see this country going to zero tolerance, period."

The Department of Transportation is already working to build the case for zero tolerance. In a recent DOT report, "Driver Characteristics and Impairment at Various BACs," the agency concludes that "a majority of the driving public is impaired in some important measures at BACs as low as .02 percent." "Finally," the report reads, "this laboratory study indicates that some important driving skills are impaired when there has been use of even small amounts of alcohol." MADD London has used the report to call for a .05 BAC limit in England.

Many jurisdictions have in fact already enacted modified zero tolerance. For example, merely registering a BAC below .08 doesn't always get a motorist off the hook. In several cities and counties across the country, police officers have the discretion to arrest drivers for "driving under the influence" if the driver merely admits to having consumed alcohol or *any* amount of alcohol is registered in a breath test. When that is combined with random sobriety checkpoints on roadways (a topic that will be discussed in more detail below), a motorist could have a beer or two, be well under .08, drive safely and responsibly, and *still* be subject to arrest for "driving under the influence" and all of the embarrassment, public disgrace, and damage to reputation that come with a criminal charge of mixing alcohol with driving.

In Florida police officers are permitted to arrest motorists they suspect are driving under the influence of alcohol, even if the motorists pass a breath test. In fact, even if a urine test later proves negative, the State Attorney's Office could still press charges, based solely on the observations of police officers administering roadside sobriety tests.

Until 1994 in Washington, DC, blowing .05 or lower was prima facie evidence that a motorist wasn't driving under the influence of alcohol. That law has since changed. Today, *any* positive reading on a breath test is enough for a police officer to consider arrest—in effect making the nation's capital a zero tolerance jurisdiction. In an op-ed, restaurant industry spokesman John Doyle writes about Willis Van Devanter, a 66-year-old man arrested at a sobriety checkpoint in Washington, DC, after admitting to having two glasses of wine with dinner. He blew .03. Such arrests rarely achieve convictions after full-blown trials, but even a simple arrest can seriously damage the reputations of public figures or ruin the careers of professionals such as teachers and school principals.

## Sobriety Roadblocks

The most vital component of NHTSA and MADD's 2002 joint "You Drink & Drive. You Lose" campaign is the establishment of "sobriety checkpoints"—a euphemism for roadblocks where police officers stop motorists without probable cause and administer breath tests. Taken together with .08 per se and the fact that some jurisdictions leave "driving under the influence" (as opposed to "driving while intoxicated") completely to the discretion of law enforcement officials at the roadblocks, random sobriety roadblocks are perhaps the most potent and far-reaching victory of the neoprohibitionist movement. According to the MADD website, 39 states plus the District of Columbia now employ sobriety roadblocks in the ongoing campaign against drinking and driving.

By their very nature, sobriety roadblocks are designed to catch motorists who aren't driving erratically enough to otherwise be caught by law enforcement. And, as the studies mentioned above indicate, the odds are that if motorists are driving with BAC levels below .10, they aren't impaired enough to be a significant threat to public safety, either.

NHTSA instructs local police departments to publicize the fact the checkpoints will be in place, a curious undertaking if the aim is to actually catch repeated hard-drinking drivers, as opposed to merely discouraging moderate drinkers from getting behind the wheel. Indeed, the staunchest proponents of sobriety roadblocks admit that their intended and primary effect is to deter the social drinker, not to actually catch drunk drivers. In its instructions to local communities, the DOT writes, "Because only a small percentage of the driving population is affected, most people will only know about sobriety checkpoints through word-of-mouth or media reports."

The problem, once again, is that roadblocks may indeed deter social drinkers, but social drinkers aren't the primary threat to public safety. What's worse, they occupy police officers and law enforcement resources that would be better spent pursuing the real threats to public safety—people who drive with BACs of .15 or higher and who are unlikely to be deterred by public relations campaigns announcing the initiation of roadblocks.

## The Constitution

Some people might wonder how it is that police can stop a car without probable cause, force a breath test, and arrest a driver for operating a car under the influence. The answer: The U.S. Supreme Court has ruled that motorists don't have Fourth Amendment rights when it comes to sobriety roadblocks. In *Michigan Department of State Police v. Sitz*, the Supreme Court overturned a Michigan Court of Appeals ruling that roadblocks violate the Fourth Amendment rights of motorists. Writing for the majority, Chief Justice William Rehnquist reasoned that the magnitude of the drunken driving problem outweighed the "slight" intrusion on motorists "briefly" stopped at sobriety roadblocks.

Part of the case Rehnquist made in determining the severity of the drunken driving problem, however, was again predicated on "alcohol-related" traffic fatalities; Rehnquist cited a claim that drunk drivers were responsible for more than 25,000 roadway deaths annually. As noted earlier, those numbers grossly overestimate the actual number of sober individuals killed by the negligence of drunk drivers, meaning that in applying his balancing test Rehnquist seriously overstated the severity of the threat drunk driving poses to public safety.

This is a clear example of how NHTSA's fudging of numbers has had real-world policy implications. In the *Sitz* case, it played a part in abrogating the Fourth Amendment rights of anyone with a driver's license. In his dissent, Justice John Paul Stevens pointed out that the net effect on highway safety of sobriety checkpoints is "infinitesimal and possibly negative." Stevens also questioned the supposedly "slight" intrusion on motorists indicated by Rehnquist, noting that "a Michigan officer who questions a motorist at a sobriety checkpoint has virtually unlimited discretion to detain the driver on the basis of the slightest suspicion."

Justice Stevens was most penetrating, however, when criticizing the majority's disinterest in acknowledging "the citizen's interest in freedom from random, announced investigatory seizures." Noting that the real aim of checkpoints is to deter drinking by people who will never be stopped at them, Stevens described the roadblocks as "elaborate, and disquieting, publicity stunts. The possibility that anybody, no matter how innocent, may be stopped for police inspection is nothing if not attention getting."

After the Supreme Court's ruling in *Sitz*, the Michigan State Supreme Court took up the case and promptly found the same sobriety roadblocks to be in violation of the state constitution. Three other state supreme courts have also found such roadblocks to be inconsistent with their state constitutions.

---

*For 20 years the courts have been carving out exemptions from constitutional safeguards when it comes to drinking and driving.*

---

Nevertheless, the *Sitz* precedent sanctioned roadblocks for any state interested in enacting them if the state supreme court would allow them. Interestingly, since *Sitz*, the Supreme Court ruled in 2000 that similar roadblocks set up to check for illicit drugs *are* in violation of the Fourth Amendment.

Interesting, but not altogether surprising. For 20 years the courts have been carving out exemptions from constitutional safeguards when it comes to drinking and driving. As noted, drunk-driving suspects have virtually no Fourth Amendment rights. Here are some other rulings to note:

- In 1983 the Supreme Court ruled that, when it comes to DUI suspects, the Fifth Amendment right against self-incrimination needs to be relaxed.

- In 1989, although the Sixth Amendment to the Constitution guarantees a jury trial for "all criminal prosecutions," the Court ruled that there is no constitutional right to a jury trial in DUI cases, as long as the defendant isn't subject to more than six months in jail.

- In 2002 the Supreme Court of Wisconsin ruled that police officers can forcibly take blood samples from people who are suspected of driving under the influence. The court concluded that such warrantless blood draws from protesting, non-consenting adults were justified because "the dissipation of alcohol in the blood stream constituted an emergency." In 1998 a 33-year-old man by the name of Terry Jones died as a result of a struggle with police officers who were trying to forcibly draw a blood sample.

As a result of those rulings, states have seized on the exemptions carved out for them by the courts at the urging of anti-alcohol groups. Forty-one states now have "administrative license revocation," meaning DUI suspects can have their licenses rescinded before any trial has taken place. Thirty-seven states have turned the Fifth Amendment safeguard against compelled self-incrimination inside out and impose *harsher* criminal penalties on those who refuse to take breath tests than on those who take them and fail. Seventeen states have passed laws making it tougher for DUI defendants to plea bargain than it is for other defendants.

What we have are legal trends that are simultaneously pushing to apply drunk-driving laws to lower and lower levels of intoxication, fewer constitutional safeguards for drunk-driving suspects, and stricter sentencing. A DUI or DWI conviction in most states can mean fines of as much as $10,000, a six-month driver's license suspension, and even jail time for a first offense. When one considers that a few drinks can lead to the arrest of a driver, the harsh penalties that follow a conviction, the looming presence of .08 per se, roadblocks, and the reduced protections available to suspects, it's easy to see how these laws, taken together, can affect the decision about having a drink on an evening out. The campaign against drunk driving is no longer a campaign against drunk driving. It has morphed into a campaign against drinking.

# 14

# Twelve-Step Programs Help Reduce Alcohol Abuse

*Mark Warnat*

*Mark Warnat is a physician assistant and a member of the Northeastern University Physician Assistant class of 2005.*

*Members of Alcoholics Anonymous (AA) come from different classes, diverse ethnic backgrounds, and both genders, but all find a common cause in working with one another to fight alcoholism. At meetings, members take turns sharing stories about how alcohol abuse has devastated their families and relationships. For those with substance abuse problems, AA offers a supportive solution. In addition to medical aid, a physician assistant should be willing to refer a patient to AA.*

The AA [Alcoholics Anonymous] meeting was held in a stuffy basement filled with circa-1970s multicolored plastic chairs lined up in neat little rows in the middle of the floor. The fluorescent lighting and the color of the walls bathed everything in a yellow hue; everyone, including me, had a somewhat jaundiced appearance. It was a nonsmoking meeting, but the pungent aroma permeating the room made it obvious that many chain-smoking alcoholics have attended meetings in this basement. The function of the two tiny windows flanking the basement was suspect since they were not designed to open and they also did not provide much light. A coffeepot endlessly percolated in the background, and almost everyone in the basement was clutching a steaming foam cup.

Mark Warnat, "One Day at a Time," *JAAPA-Journal of the American Academy of Physician Assistants*, vol. 18, January 2005, pp. 54–55. Copyright 2005 Advanstar Communications, Inc. Reproduced by permission.

The first thing that stood out is that no fewer than 40 people were attending this meeting—a meeting happening in the middle of the day, on a random Tuesday, in a midsize suburb of Boston. They appeared to represent a cross section of society. They were men and women, black and white, tall and short, fat and thin, young and old. Some wore suits, crisp white shirts, paisley ties, and silk vests. Some had dirt under their fingernails and torn jeans. Some looked like the stereotypical alcoholic—strung out, unkempt, constantly fidgeting, tapping their feet, shifting in their chairs. But others looked as calm and cool as the other side of the pillow, with everything seemingly under control.

At this point I came to my own sobering realization—the first of several I would have that day—that we all have the potential to become better healers if we can eliminate our own preconceived notions and prejudices about patients based on their outward appearance.

## Paul's Story

This particular meeting, according to the booklet I received in the mail from Alcoholics Anonymous, was designated as an open speaker session. In the front of the room, behind a rickety metal desk, sat a middle-aged man wearing an Aeropostale sweatshirt and a baseball cap. His midsection was a bit pudgy, a striking contrast to the gaunt face.

Peering out from behind the curled brim of his cap, he began the meeting in the customary way: "Hi," he said. "I'm Paul, and I'm an alcoholic." The reply—"Hi, Paul!"—was quick and amplified from his one voice to our 40.

Paul started off by saying that he was nervous since this was the first time he had ever led a meeting. Paul's voice quivered, either from nerves or as a side effect of choking back the sadness that alcoholism had thrust upon his life. Probably it was from a bit of both. He told us how in 1999, after one of his usual drinking binges, he blacked out and lost an entire day. He described how from that day on, he battled the disease of alcoholism by attending up to six AA meetings a day. He mentioned how much he needed these meetings because alcohol and drug abuse had alienated him from his family. He spoke of how much he missed his wife and children and how he hoped that, over time, they would be reintegrated into his newly established world of sobriety.

Throughout his gut-wrenching speech, Paul took full responsibility for his circumstances. He didn't blame anyone— not his wife, his children, his former boss, Sam Adams, Jose Cuervo, Captain Morgan, Osama Bin Laden, God, or the economy. He was contrite. He blamed himself, and he was trying his best to make amends for the wrongs he had done and to slay his personal demons.

## Celebrating Sobriety

Paul talked for about 15 minutes before opening the floor to other attendees. Seven people used the remainder of the hour to tell their own stories. Each had an equally awful tale of how the bottle, the needle, or the pill case led to their downfall. Some finished their monologue on a happy note, speaking of redemption and blissful reunions. Others did not.

---

*Alcoholics Anonymous does indeed work for people with addictions to alcohol and other substances of abuse. . . .*

---

After the open forum came an announcement that the group would now give brightly colored poker chips to those who had been able to go a certain period of time without abusing. These chips were small trinkets to mark a milestone in sobriety. The chip itself was worth a fraction of a penny, yet what it represented was invaluable. "Nine months . . . nine months . . ." was yelled out. Two women walked to the front of the room and, sheepishly yet proudly, grabbed the little plastic representation of their hard work. Everyone in the room cheered exuberantly. "Six months?" came next. "Six months? . . . Three months? . . . Two months? . . . Two months? . . ." Yet nobody stood to receive a chip. After a moment, the speaker continued: "Finally, and perhaps most important of all, 24 hours without a drink?" One woman stood, grabbed the token without making eye contact with anyone in the room, and quickly sat back in her seat, squirreling away her prized possession. She got the most rousing round of applause of all.

When the room finally settled down, the speaker asked one final question. "To prove that AA and these meetings work, can we get a show of hands from those who have been clean and sober for a year or more?" Over half of the attendees raised a hand, and more sounds of applause spread through the room.

At this point I had my second sobering realization. Alcoholics Anonymous does indeed work for people with addictions to alcohol and other substances of abuse, and the phone number for the nearest AA support group is a tool that PAs should consider as important as our ophthalmoscope or stethoscope. Local AA contact numbers should be a part of the vigilant clinician's repertoire, as it is our duty to find every possible resource and offer it to those in need.

As I think back on this experience, what really stands out is how accepting the people at this meeting were of each other. It is almost tragically beautiful that without hesitation, young embraced old, black embraced white, straight embraced gay, and all the categories and differences that segregate people in the "real world" melted away in that dirty, smelly basement. These strangers who shared this disease called alcoholism, who shared this awful experience, who shared this addiction and the pain that always accompanies it, seemed no longer to see race, creed, or color when looking at their fellow addicts. The outer shell that usually defines a person was stripped away, leaving a simple common core of someone battling to stay sober, one day at a time. These people were not looking for miracles. They were not looking to take giants leaps. They were simply looking to live life on life's terms while resisting the urge to escape into the bottom of a bottle.

# 15

# Twelve-Step Programs Seldom Reduce Alcohol Abuse

*Salvador Sanchez*

*Salvador Sanchez worked as the business manager for the* Western Herald, *a newspaper serving college campuses in Kalamazoo, Michigan.*

*Alcoholics Anonymous (AA) is often presented as the best solution for curing alcoholism but the program is old-fashioned and may not be right for everyone. While AA calls alcoholism an incurable and involuntary disease, the U.S. Supreme Court has said that there is no validating medical basis for defining alcoholism as such. Despite the faulty logic of AA's core beliefs, employers force employees and courts force citizens to attend meetings. The fact that AA openly characterizes itself as a religious organization further complicates forced attendance by violating the U.S. Constitution's religious freedom clause in the First Amendment. Finally, the biggest problem with AA is that it has a very low success rate. It is true that AA does work for some people, but there are other organizations that should also be recognized as supportive for those with substance abuse problems.*

Alcoholics Anonymous is not the only way. Originally founded in 1935, a couple of years after the Prohibition fiasco of the 1920s and 1930s, Alcoholics Anonymous became a non-professional organization. For decades they have advocated their 12-step program that so many have embraced and followed.

Salvador Sanchez, "Alcoholics Anonymous Not Always Best Solution," *Western Herald*, September 1, 2004. Reproduced by permission.

With the help of God and admission of the exact nature of wrongs, people are supposed to have a spiritual awakening. This is, by all means, a great theory, but in some aspects it is just that—a theory.

First of all, this is a procedure that is supposed to undeniably work for people. There have been no changes or advancements to this 12-step program since its inception. How confident can a person feel when someone is telling them that they are going to get them through this rough time, using a 70-year-old method with no real records to prove the efficacy? Should people let doctors treat symptoms and maladies with methods that were used in the '30s? The answer is no; technology and science are here to help advance archaic ways and to further our growth as a society—so let it be done.

In fact, many say that alcoholism is a disease and this is a cure. This, in fact, was a huge belief by the founders of AA, who believed these views because of their own observations, religious ideas, experiences and unsubstantiated theories.

The Supreme Court has fought battles with regard to this before, when they concluded that medical evidence does not demonstrate drinking as involuntary. In the *Trainer v. Turnage* case they even went as far as to call alcoholism "willful misconduct."

So, how can this be a disease when it is done because of the behavior of a human being? It is an addiction, created by a behavior and spawned from a choice. Therefore, if this 12-step program does work for this disease, why in the world don't we use an equivalent to the greatness of this idea to help cure the disease called cancer?

Science is not the only issue here. Insanity is often defined as doing the same thing repeatedly and expecting different results; thus, doesn't insanity play a small role here? Individuals repeatedly attending a meeting expecting a different result, when the numbers to support that Alcoholics Anonymous works are non-existent, seem to be bordering on this definition of insanity.

## Politics and Religion

Next, Alcoholics Anonymous, on its own Web site, claims to be apolitical, yet in many cases across the nation the U.S. government mandates individuals to participate in this. How can this be apolitical? Employers will tell employees that they have to attend AA to keep their job. People are setting stipulations onto others, with the end result being attendance at a non-professional organization. An organization that reports it keeps no case histories, no follow-up on their participants, and no letters of reference for individuals who endured the steps and the infamous quote, "Hi, I am John and I am an alcoholic."

Furthermore, this organization that courts and employers send men and women to embraces God and religion. The Supreme Law of the Land itself states in its Bill of Rights that everyone is entitled to freedom of and from religion. This has to include atheists and Buddhists; thus, to embrace God leaves little room for both parties.

Finally, since Alcoholics Anonymous does little with case studies, few can find more recent studies than a 1989 survey done by Alcoholics Anonymous that found that only 5 percent of those that went to Alcoholics Anonymous were able to say they no longer drank. Ironically, this same survey found that among the U.S. population, 5 percent of alcoholics who quit could say they remained sober—impressive, outdated numbers.

This is not to say that Alcoholics Anonymous and the 12-step program do not work. I am sure that it works for some. We all know someone or someone who knows someone that has made it out of AA as a recovering alcoholic; this is just to say that it is not the only way. There are other avenues that should be considered.

S.O.S., or Secular Organizations for Sobriety/Save Our Selves, is an alternative to AA. S.O.S. was founded in 1985 after the founder no longer believed in the answer AA was offering him. Today, there are 20,000 members and several courts have recognized this organization as an alternative to the commercialized Alcoholics Anonymous.

Another option is an FDA-approved oral antagonist against the action of opiates called naltrexone. The FDA actually approves naltrexone for the treatment of alcohol dependence.

I could end by saying that Alcoholics Anonymous is government-mandated, religious nonsense; however, I will end with this: Alcoholics Anonymous does work. It obviously does not work for everyone, but there are other options than AA. In a way, this once-innovative organization has become commercialized and lost its original notoriety; therefore, it is important to point out some of the small things.

# Organizations to Contact

*The editors have compiled the following list of organizations concerned with the issues debated in this book. The descriptions are derived from materials provided by the organizations. All have publications or information available for interested readers. The list was compiled on the date of publication of the present volume; the information provided here may change. Be aware that many organizations take several weeks or longer to respond to inquiries, so allow as much time as possible.*

## Al-Anon Family Group Headquarters
1600 Corporate Landing Pkwy.
Virginia Beach, VA   23454-5617
(757) 563-1600 • fax: (757) 563-1655
We bsite: www.al-anon.alateen.org

Al-Anon is a fellowship of men, women, and children whose lives have been affected by an alcoholic family member or friend. Members share their experiences, strength, and hope to help each other and perhaps to aid in the recovery of the alcoholic. Al-Anon Family Group Headquarters provides information on its local chapters and on its affiliated organization, Alateen. Its publications include the monthly magazine the *Forum*, the semiannual *Al-Anon Speaks Out*, the bimonthly *Alateen Talk*, and several books, including *How Al-Anon Works, Path to Recovery: Steps, Traditions, and Concepts*, and *Courage to Be Me: Living with Alcoholism*.

## Alcoholics Anonymous (AA)
General Service Office, New York, NY   10163
(212) 870-3400 • fax: (212) 870-3003
Web site: www.aa.org

Alcoholics Anonymous is an international fellowship of people who are recovering from alcoholism. Because AA's primary goal is to help alcoholics remain sober, it does not sponsor research or engage in education about alcoholism. AA does publish a catalog of literature concerning the organization, as well as several pamphlets, including *Is AA for You? Young People and AA*, and *A Brief Guide to Alcoholics Anonymous*.

### American Beverage Institute (ABI)
American Beverage Institute, Washington, DC   20005
(202) 463-7110
Web site: www.abionline.org

The American Beverage Institute is a restaurant industry trade organization that works to protect the consumption of alcoholic beverages in the restaurant setting. It unites the wine, beer, and spirits producers with distributors and on-premise retailers in this effort. It conducts research and education in an attempt to demonstrate that the vast majority of adults who drink alcohol outside of the home are responsible, law-abiding citizens. Its Web site includes fact sheets and news articles on various issues, such as drunk-driving laws and alcohol taxes, and research reports including "The Anti-Drunk Driving Campaign: A Covert War Against Drinking" and "The .08 Debate: What's the Harm?"

### American Council on Science and Health (ACSH)
1995 Broadway, 2nd Fl., New York, NY   10023-5860
(212) 362-7044 • fax: (212) 362-4919
e-mail: acsh@acsh.org
Web site: www.acsh.org

ACSH is a consumer education group concerned with issues related to food, nutrition, chemicals, pharmaceuticals, lifestyle, the environment, and health. It publishes the quarterly newsletter *Priorities* as well as the booklets *The Tobacco Industry's Use of Nicotine as a Drug* and *A Comparison of the Health Effects of Alcohol Consumption and Tobacco Use in America*.

### American Society of Addiction Medicine (ASAM)
4601 N. Park Ave., Upper Arcade #101
Chevy Chase, MD   20815

(301) 656-3920 • fax: (301) 656-3815
e-mail: email@asam.org
Web site: www.asam.org

ASAM is the nation's addiction medicine specialty society dedicated to educating physicians and improving the treatment of individuals suffering from alcoholism and other addictions. In addition, the organization promotes research and prevention of addiction and works for the establishment of addiction medicine as a specialty recognized by the American Board of Medical Specialties. The organization publishes medical texts and a bimonthly newsletter.

**The Beer Institute**
122 C St. NW, Ste. 750, Washington, DC    20001
(202) 737-2337 • fax: (202) 737-7004
e-mail: info@beerinstitute.org
Web site: www.beerinstitute.org

The Beer Institute is a trade organization that represents the beer industry before Congress, state legislatures, and public forums across the country. It sponsors educational programs to prevent underage drinking and drunk driving and distributes fact sheets and news briefs on issues such as alcohol taxes and advertising. Its *Beer Institute Bulletin* newsletter is published four times a year.

**Canadian Centre on Substance Abuse/Centre canadien de lutte contre l'alcoolisme et les toxicomanies (CCSA/CCLAT)**
75 Albert St., Ste. 300, Ottawa, ON   K1P 5E7
   Canada
(613) 235-4048 • fax: (613) 235-8101
Web site: www.ccsa.ca

A Canadian clearinghouse on substance abuse, the CCSA/CCLAT works to disseminate information on the nature, extent, and consequences of substance abuse and to support and assist organizations involved in substance abuse treatment, prevention, and educational programming. The CCSA/CCLAT publishes several books, including *Canadian Profile: Alcohol, Tobacco, and Other Drugs*, as well as reports, policy documents, brochures, research papers, and the newsletter *Action News*.

**Center for Science in the Public Interest (CSPI)**
1875 Connecticut Ave. NW, Ste. 300, Washington, DC 20009
(202) 332-9110 • fax: (202) 265-4954
e-mail: cspi@cspinet.org
Web site: www.cspinet.org

CSPI is an advocacy organization that promotes nutrition and health, food safety, alcohol policy, and sound science. It favors the implementation of public policies aimed at reducing alcohol-related problems, such as restricting on alcohol advertising and increasing alcohol taxes. CSPI publishes the monthly *Nutrition Action Healthletter*, and its Web site contains fact sheets and reports on alcohol-related problems and alcohol policies.

**Centre for Addiction and Mental Health/Centre de toxicomanie et de santé mentale (CAMH)**
33 Russell St., Toronto, ON M5S 2S1
  Canada
(416) 535-8501 ext. 6878
Web site: www.camh.net

CAMH is a public hospital and the largest addiction facility in Canada. It also functions as a research facility, an education and training center, and a community-based organization providing health and addiction prevention services throughout Ontario, Canada. Further, CAMH is a Pan American Health Organization and World Health Organization Collaborating Centre. CAMH publishes the quarterly *CrossCurrents, the Journal of Addiction and Mental Health* and offers free alcoholism prevention literature that can either be downloaded or ordered on the Web site.

## Century Council

1310 G St., NW, Ste. 600, Washington, DC   20005
(202) 637-0077 • fax: (202) 637-0079
e-mail: moultone@centurycouncil.org
Web site: www.centurycouncil.org

A nonprofit organization funded by America's liquor industry, the Century Council's mission is to fight drunk driving and underage drinking. It seeks to promote responsible decision-making about drinking and discourage all forms of irresponsible alcohol consumption through education, communications, research, law enforcement, and other programs. It's Web site offers fact sheets and other resources on drunk driving, underage drinking, and other alcohol-related problems.

## Distilled Spirits Council of the United States (DISCUS)

1250 I St. NW, Ste. 900, Washington, DC   20005
(202) 628-3544
Web site: www.discus.org

The Distilled Spirits Council of the United States is the national trade association representing producers and marketers of distilled spirits in the United States. It seeks to ensure the responsible advertising and marketing of distilled spirits to adult consumers and to prevent such advertising and marketing from targeting individuals below the legal purchase age. DISCUS publishes fact sheets, news releases, and documents, including its "Code of Responsible Practices for Beverage Alcohol Advertising and Marketing."

## International Center for Alcohol Policies (ICAP)

1519 New Hampshire Ave. NW, Washington, DC   20036
(202) 986-1159 • fax: (202) 986-2080
Web site: www.icap.org

The International Center for Alcohol Policies is a nonprofit organization dedicated to helping reduce the abuse of alcohol worldwide and to promote understanding of the role of alcohol in society through dialogue and partnerships involving the beverage industry, the public health community and others interested in alcohol policy. ICAP is supported by eleven major international beverage alcohol companies. ICAP publishes reports on pertinent issues such as *Safe Alcohol Consumption, The Limits of Binge Drinking, Health Warning Labels, Drinking Age Limits, What Is a "Standard Drink"?, Government Policies on Alcohol and Pregnancy, Estimating Costs Associated with Alcohol Abuse,* and *Who Are the Abstainers?*

**The Marin Institute**
24 Belvedere St., San Rafael, CA 94901
(415) 456-5692 • fax: (415) 456-0491
Web site: www.marininstitute.org

The Marin Institute works to reduce alcohol problems by improving our physical and social environment to advance public health and safety. The institute promotes stricter alcohol policies—including higher taxes—in order to reduce alcohol-related problems. It publishes fact sheets and news alerts on alcohol policy, advertising, and other alcohol-related issues. Its "Talk Back System" allows users of its Web site to complain directly to the alcohol industry about irresponsible advertising and marketing practices.

**Mothers Against Drunk Driving (MADD)**
511 E. John Carpenter Frwy., Ste. 700, Irving, TX 75062
800-GET-MADD (438-6233) • fax: (972) 869-2206/07
e-mail: information: info@madd.org
Web site: www.madd.org

Mothers Against Drunk Driving seeks to act as the voice of victims of drunk-driving accidents by speaking on their behalf to communities, businesses, and educational groups and by providing materials for use in medical facilities and health and driver education programs. MADD publishes the biannual *MADDvocate for Victims Magazine* and the newsletter *MADD in Action* as well as a variety of fact sheets, brochures, and other materials on drunk driving.

## National Center on Addiction and Substance Abuse (CASA)
633 Third Ave., 19th Fl., New York, NY   10017-6706
(212) 841-5200
Web site: www.casacolumbia.org

CASA is a nonprofit organization affiliated with Columbia University. It works to educate the public about the problems of substance abuse and addiction and evaluate prevention, treatment, and law enforcement programs to address the problem. Its Web site contains reports and op-ed articles on alcohol policy and the alcohol industry, including the reports *Teen Tipplers: America's Underage Drinking Epidemic* and *The Economic Value of Underage and Adult Excessive Drinking to the Alcohol Industry.*

## National Council on Alcoholism and Drug Dependence (NCADD)
244 East 58th St., 4th Fl., New York, NY   10022
(212) 269-7797 • fax: (212) 269-7510
e-mail: national@ncadd.org
Web site: www.ncadd.org

NCADD is a volunteer health organization that helps individuals overcome addictions, advises the federal government on drug and alcohol policies, and develops substance abuse prevention and education programs for youth. It publishes fact sheets, such as *Youth and Alcohol*, and pamphlets, such as *Who's Got the Power? You . . . Or Drugs?*

## National Highway Traffic Safety Administration (NHTSA)
400 Seventh St. SW, Washington, DC   20590
(888) 327-4236

The NHTSA is the division of the U.S. Department of Transportation that is responsible for reducing deaths, injuries, and economic losses resulting from motor vehicle crashes. It sets and enforces safety performance standards for motor vehicles and motor vehicle equipment and awards grants to state and local governments to enable them to conduct local highway safety programs. The NHTSA publishes information on drunk driving, including *Get the Keys* and *Strategies for Success: Combating Juvenile DUI.*

### National Institute on Alcohol Abuse and Alcoholism (NIAAA)
5635 Fishers Lane, MSC 9304, Bethesda, MD   20892-9304
(301) 443-3860
Web site: www.niaaa.nih.gov

The National Institute on Alcohol Abuse and Alcoholism is one of the eighteen institutes that comprise the National Institutes of Health. NIAAA provides leadership in the national effort to reduce alcohol-related problems. NIAAA is an excellent source of information and publishes the quarterly bulletin, *Alcohol Alert;* a quarterly scientific journal, *Alcohol Research and Health;* and many pamphlets, brochures, and posters dealing with alcohol abuse and alcoholism. All of these publications, including NIAAA's congressional testimony, are available online.

### Rational Recovery Systems (RRS)
PO Box 800, Lotus, CA   95651
(530) 621-2667 • (530) 621-4374
e-mail: rrsn@rational.org
Web site: www.rational.org/recovery

RRS is a national self-help organization that offers a cognitive rather than spiritual approach to recovery from alcoholism. Its philosophy holds that alcoholics can attain sobriety without depending on other people or a "higher power." Rational Recovery Systems publishes materials about the organization and its use of rational-emotive therapy.

### Research Society on Alcoholism (RSA)
7801 N. Lamar Blvd., Ste. D-89, Austin, TX   78752-1038
(512) 454-0022 • fax: (512) 454-0812
e-mail: debbyrsa@bga.com
Web site: www.rsoa.org

The RSA provides a forum for researchers who share common interests in alcoholism. The society's purpose is to promote research on the prevention and treatment of alcoholism. It publishes the journal *Alcoholism: Clinical and Experimental Research* nine times a year as well as the book series Recent Advances in Alcoholism.

**Secular Organizations for Sobriety (SOS)**
4773 Hollywood Blvd., Hollywood, CA   90027
(323) 666-4295 • Fax: (323) 666-4271
e-mail: SOS@CFIWest.org
Web site: www.secularsobriety.org

SOS is a network of groups dedicated to helping individuals achieve and maintain sobriety. The organization believes that alcoholics can best recover by rationally choosing to make sobriety rather than alcohol a priority. Most members of SOS reject the spiritual basis of Alcoholics Anonymous and other similar self-help groups. SOS publishes the quarterly *SOS International Newsletter* and distributes the books *Unhooked: Staying Sober and Drug Free* and *How to Stay Sober: Recovery Without Religion*, written by SOS founder James Christopher.

**Substance Abuse and Mental Health
Services Administration (SAMSA)**
1 Choke Cherry Road, Rockville, MD   20847
(800) 729-6686 • fax: (301) 230-2867
Web site: www.health.org

SAMSA is a division of the U.S. Department of Health and Human Services that is responsible for improving the lives of those with or at risk for mental illness or substance addiction. Through the NCADI, SAMSA provides the public with a wide variety of information on alcoholism and other addictions. Its publications include the bimonthly *Prevention Pipeline*, the fact sheet *Alcohol Alert*, monographs such as "Social Marketing/ Media Advocacy" and "Advertising and Alcohol," brochures, pamphlets, videotapes, and posters. Publications in Spanish are also available.

# Bibliography

## Books

Henry Abraham
*What's a Parent to Do?: Straight Talk on Drugs and Alcohol.* Liberty Corner, NJ: New Horizon, 2004.

Caroline Jean Acker and Sarah W. Tracy
*Altering American Consciousness: The History of Alcohol and Drug Use in the United States, 1800-2000.* Amherst, MA: University of Massachusetts Press, 2004.

Rosalyn Carson-DeWitt
*Encyclopedia of Drugs, Alcohol & Addictive Behavior.* New York: MacMillan Reference, 2001.

Susan Cheever
*My Name Is Bill: Bill Wilson—His Life and the Creation of Alcoholics Anonymous.* New York: Simon & Schuster, 2004.

Patt Denning
*Over the Influence: The Harm Reduction Guide for Managing Drugs and Alcohol.* New York: Guilford, 2004.

Constance M. Horgan
*Substance Abuse: The Nation's Number One Health Problem.* Princeton, NJ: The Foundation, 2001.

Devon Jersild
*Happy Hours: Alcohol in a Woman's Life.* New York: Cliff Street Books, 2001.

Cynthia Kuhn, Scott Swatzwelder, and Wilkie Wilson
*Buzzed: The Straight Facts About the Most Used and Abused Drugs from Alcohol to Ecstasy.* New York: W.W. Norton, 2003.

Cynthia Kuhn, Scott Swatzwelder, and Wilkie Wilson
*Just Say Know: Talking With Kids About Drugs and Alcohol.* New York: W.W. Norton, 2002.

Francis Mark Mondimore
*Adolescent Depression: A Guide for Parents.* Baltimore, MD: Johns Hopkins University Press, 2002.

Peter M. Monti and Suzanne M. Colby
*Adolescents, Alcohol, and Substance Abuse: Reaching Teens Through Brief Interventions.* New York: Guilford, 2001.

Barry Stimmel
*Alcoholism, Drug Addiction, and the Road to Recovery: Life on the Edge.* New York: Haworth Medical, 2002.

Stuart Walton
*Out of It: A Cultural History of Intoxication.* New York: Harmony, 2002.

Henry Wechsler and Bernice Wuethrich
*Dying to Drink: Confronting Binge Drinking on College Campuses.* New York: St. Martin's, 2002.

Koren Zailckas
*Smashed: Story of a Drunken Girlhood.* New York: Viking, 2005.

## Periodicals

Susan Brink
"A Closer Look: Alcoholism—All Part of Managing a Disease," *Los Angeles Times*, August 14, 2006.

Katy Butler   "The Grim Neurology of Teenage Drinking," *New York Times*, July 4, 2006.

Larry Copeland  "Some See Fresno's DUI Crackdown as a Model," *USA Today*, November 5, 2006.

Benoit Denizet-Lewis "Ban of Brothers," *New York Times Magazine*, January 9, 2005.

Randy Dotinga  "Quandary for Colleges: How to Battle Binge Drinking," *Christian Science Monitor*, January 18, 2005.

Jane Glenn Haas "Alcohol Abuse Has No Age Limit," *Orange County Register*, May 23, 2006.

Connie Lauerman "Three Women Chronicle Their Battles with Alcoholism," *Chicago Tribune*, November 10, 2003.

Jodie Morse   "Women on a Binge," *Time*, April 1, 2002.

National Institute on Alcohol Abuse and Alcoholism "Alcohol's Damaging Effects on the Brain," *Alcohol Alert*, no. 63, October 2004.

National Institute on Alcohol Abuse and Alcoholism "The Scope of the Problem," *Alcohol Research & Health*, vol. 28, no. 3, 2004–2005.

National Institute on Alcohol Abuse and Alcoholism "Surgeon General Calls on Americans to Face Facts About Drinking," *NIH News Release*, April 1, 2004.

| | |
|---|---|
| National Survey on Drug Use and Health | "Gender Differences in Substance Dependence and Abuse," *The NSDUH Report*, October 29, 2004. |
| Stanton Peele | "The Surprising Truth About Addiction," *Psychology Today*, May–June 2004. |
| Helen Phillips and Graham Lawton | "The Intoxication Instinct," *New Scientist*, November 13, 2004. |
| Jim Rankin and Joseph Hall | "Over the Limit: Who Are the Drunk Drivers?" *Toronto Star*, May 17, 2003. |
| Shari Roan | "Threat Behind the Party-Girl Image," *Los Angeles Times*, May 8, 2006. |
| Rita Rubin | "1 in 5 Adults Say a Family Member Is an Addict," *USA Today*, July 19, 2006. |
| Tina Hesman Saey | "Drug Use Can Damage the Brain, Lead to Addiction," *St. Louis Post-Dispatch*, April 2, 2006. |
| Karen Springen and Barbara Kantrowitz | "Alcohol's Deadly Triple Threat," *Newsweek*, May 10, 2004. |
| Scott H. Stewart and Gerard J. Connors | "Screening for Alcohol Problems: What Makes a Test Effective?," *Alcohol Research & Health*, vol. 28, no. 1, 2004–2005. |
| Aaron M. White | "What Happened? Alcohol, Memory Blackouts, and the Brain," *Alcohol Research & Health*, vol. 27, no. 2, 2003. |

Kate Zernike          "A 21st-Birthday Drinking Game Can
                      Be a Deadly Rite of Passage," *New
                      York Times*, March 12, 2005.

## Internet Sources

Just-Drinks.com       "Magazine Alcohol Ads Hit Underage
                      Girls," *Just-Drinks.com*, July 6, 2004.
                      www.just-drinks.com.

# Index